PRAISE FOR SHATTERED

"In *Shattered*, Gary Roe utilizes the stories and journeys of many bereaved parents to walk the reader from shock to hope. Gary is no stranger to the reality of grief and utilizes his unique empathy and understanding gained though a lifetime of working with the bereaved to create a truly healing book."

—Glen Lord, President/CEO, The Grief Toolbox; President, National Board of Directors, The Compassionate Friends, father of Noah Thomas Emory Lord, who died at age 4½

"Few people truly comprehend the unique and challenging grief experiences of bereaved parents. Yet Gary Roe not only understands but also offers hope, healing, and compassion from a Christian perspective. As a bereaved parent and also as a professional who has worked with bereaved parents, I would highly recommend *Shattered*."

—Peggy Telg, Independent Bereavement Educator, mother of Michael and Christopher, who died in infancy

"*Shattered* is a sensitive, compassionate, and thorough treatment of an extremely emotional and difficult subject. Bereaved parents and grandparents everywhere will benefit from this heartfelt book and find some healing and hope in its pages. I would highly recommend this book for groups as well."

— Paul Casale, Licensed Marriage & Family
Therapist and Mental Health Counselor

"There isn't a book that can be written to explain exactly how we feel, but *Shattered* is no doubt the closest I've seen. This book doesn't only apply to those who've lost a child, but can also help those who are dealing with a friend or family member who has lost a child. Thanks to Gary Roe for helping us speak and giving our shattered lives a voice."

— Michelle Jeter, author of *A Legacy of a Lifetime*
and mother of Sydney, who died at age 16

"In *Shattered*, Gary Roe uniquely and delicately addresses the devastating subject of losing a child. This book will be an excellent resource, not only for bereaved parents, but also for those who support them."

— Joangeli Kasper, Licensed Professional Counselor

"Your grief will be unique because your child was unique. Nevertheless, you will find something helpful in *Shattered*. Gary offers tons of practical advice about moving through this challenging time."

— Cherry Moore, hospice chaplain, artist, and mother of Lew, who died at age 16

"There's nothing more devastating and painful in life than the loss of a child. The challenge of living life after such an event is staggering. *Shattered* is a source of compassionate insight into a truly difficult topic, the handiwork of Gary Roe's efforts to bring hope and healing."

— Dr. Craig Borchardt, President/ CEO, Hospice Brazos Valley

"*Shattered* is superb. I believe that anyone could read it and find help with their grief after losing a child. It is a thorough, timely, and much needed book that could also be used as an excellent grief counseling reference manual."

— Dr. Tony Taylor, Senior Pastor, Hilltop Lakes Chapel

"As a mental health professional for three decades, I find great value in Gary's presentation of one of the toughest clinical issues to deal with in therapy. Most adults verbalize the loss of a child as one of their top fears. I will keep several copies on hand for families or support folks walking this difficult journey."

— Carrie Andree, Licensed Professional Counselor

"When my 4-day old Allie died with Trisomy 18, I was numb, sad, and then angry. This book helped me work through each stage of my feelings. I thought I was going crazy and that I would never be the same again. As I was reading *Shattered*, I started feeling that my mental state was justifiable. It is truly a book of healing!"

— Ronna Prickett, mother of Allie, who died in infancy

SHATTERED

Surviving the Loss of a Child

Gary Roe

CONTENTS

OTHER BOOKS
BY GARY ROE

*Please Be Patient, I'm Grieving: How to Care
For and Support the Grieving Heart*
(2016 USA Best Book Awards Finalist)

HEARTBROKEN: Healing from the Loss of a Spouse
(2015 USA Best Book Awards Finalist, National
Indie Excellence Book Awards Finalist)

*Surviving the Holidays Without You: Navi-
gating Grief During Special Seasons*
(2016 Book Excellence Awards Finalist)

(co-authored with Cecil Murphey)

Saying Goodbye: Facing the Loss of a Loved One

*Not Quite Healed: 40 Truths for Male Sur-
vivors of Childhood Sexual Abuse*
(2013 Lime Award Finalist for Excellence in Non-Fiction)

ACKNOWLEDGMENTS

Special thanks to Anni Welbourne, Kathy Trim of TEAM Japan, and Kelli Levey of Texas A&M for their expertise and assistance in editing and proofing this manuscript.

Thanks to fellow hospice chaplain Cherry Moore and bereavement educator Peggy Telg for their invaluable feedback and input.

Thanks to Hospice Brazos Valley President and CEO Dr. Craig Borchardt for his support and encouragement in developing resources to help grieving people recover, adjust, and heal.

Thanks to Glendon Haddix of Streetlight Graphics for bringing this manuscript to life with superb design and formatting.

OPENING REMARKS:

WHAT THIS BOOK IS ALL ABOUT

THE LOSS OF A CHILD is a terrible thing.

Unthinkable, unbelievable, and heartbreaking. Devastating, shocking, and crushing. Paralyzing, shattering, and traumatic. These are a few of the words grieving parents have shared with me. Whatever words we choose, they all fall far short of the reality.

How do we survive this? Can we?

WHY I WROTE THIS BOOK

For several years, people have been asking me to write this resource. Honestly, I didn't want to. The mere thought of it terrified me. The death of a child is such a tender, emotionally power-packed subject. Deep in my heart, I was afraid that I would fail and somehow make things even worse.

So I kept putting the idea on the back burner saying, "Maybe one day."

About a year ago, a hospice colleague I deeply respect pulled me aside and challenged me. "You have to write this book," she said. She had lost two children herself. I began to seriously pray about it.

Over the next several months, I kept encountering grieving parents — many more than usual. I received dozens of requests in person and online. "Help! Please write some-

1

thing for us." I referred parents to organizations, other authors, and many excellent resources. Yet, the pleas kept coming.

Finally, I gave in.

What you have in your hand or on your screen is the result of three decades' experience as a missionary, pastor, and hospice chaplain, interacting with hundreds of parents who have lost children. I've also conducted over 150 interviews of grieving parents over the last year. Hearing these stories and compiling this book has been one of the most intense emotional projects in which I have ever been involved.

WHAT READERS CAN EXPECT

What will readers get from this book?

First, this book is not a magic pill. This cannot be fixed. There are no easy answers. To some things, there may be no answers at all.

Secondly, the loss of a child affects everything. I mean everything. It impacts all of us, our whole person—emotionally, mentally, physically, spiritually, and relationally. It alters the present and the future.

As a result, I've divided this book into six parts:

- The Emotional Impact
- The Mental Impact
- The Physical Impact
- The Spiritual Impact
- The Relational Impact
- The Future Impact

Chapters are purposefully brief, easy-to-read, and practical. In each story, the names have been changed to protect the privacy of those involved. Each chapter concludes with a statement that expresses what many are feeling during this grief process, along with some questions to consider or an exercise to try. Intellectually understanding grief is one thing. Processing and moving through it is another. This book was written to facilitate both.

The overall goal is to help parents grieve in healthy and responsible ways. This includes:

- Managing the massive changes that are occurring in your life
- Taking care of yourself during this process
- Honoring your child with your grief
- Loving those around you, even with a broken heart
- Living life as well as possible in the midst of great pain
- Making your child's life count in deep and powerful ways

SOME PERSONAL NOTES...

Please know this: I haven't figured this grief thing out. I don't see myself as further along than anyone else in any category. At best, I'm a fellow struggler. I tussle regularly with emotional, mental, physical, and spiritual issues stemming from the losses I have endured and encounter daily.

As I write this, I see myself walking alongside you in the valley of grief. I can't pretend to know how you feel or the depth of your pain. I want to meet you where you are and learn with you, and from you. I consider this a great honor and privilege.

This is one of the positive miracles of the grief process.

Though we're all different and our losses are all unique, we can still walk together. Thank goodness. We need each other. Desperately.

My prayer is that this book will be comforting, encouraging, and hope-giving. I hope your heart finds it so.

Before you read on, allow me to assure you of three things. Read them slowly. Let them sink in.

1. You are not alone, though an overwhelming loneliness might seize you at any given moment.

2. You are not crazy, but losing a child will make you think you are.

3. You can survive this, though many times you might wonder how.

Breathe deeply. This is a tough, hard journey. I'm honored to be traveling with you.

Gary Roe
January 2017

PART ONE:

The Emotional Impact

AT FIRST, WE'RE SHOCKED. WE'RE stunned, perhaps even emotionally paralyzed. We blink, and wonder what happened.

Waves of emotion come crashing in. We're sad. We're angry. We feel guilty, anxious, fearful, and depressed. We're frustrated and confused. Panic descends at times. We feel lost and alone.

Nothing is as it was. Everything seems surreal.

In this section, we'll be talking about the incredible emotional impact of our loss. How do we handle the powerful onslaught of feelings? Is it possible to manage them in a healthy way? If so, how?

Breathe deeply, and read on...

CHAPTER 1

SHOCK: "THIS CAN'T BE REAL!"

> *"The only education in grief that any of*
> *us ever gets is a crash course."*
>
> — *Gail Calwell*

"THIS ISN'T HAPPENING! THIS CAN'T be real!" Carla said, as she sat in the family area outside the Emergency Room.

"One moment she's here. The next, she's gone. How can this be?" she asked frantically.

Carla blinked. Her eyes took on a glazed appearance. She looked past me, staring at the blank wall by the door.

Carla was in shock.

Carla's daughter Carrie was six weeks old when she died. She had just started to coo. SIDS robbed Carla and her husband David of their precious little girl.

No wonder Carla was in shock. How could she not be?

AN EMOTIONAL TASER

When loss hits the heart, we're stunned. Like an emotional taser, sudden shock waves immobilize us.

Shock can be a good thing. It acts to shield us from the full onslaught of reality. Otherwise the blow might kill us.

When we first hear the news, time stops. It's like someone pushed the pause button on the universe. Our hearts reel. Our minds spin.

No. This cannot be happening. This cannot be real.

Shock is normal. The loss of a child is like being hit by an unexpected tsunami. It knocks us senseless. Shock can be momentary, or last for days or weeks.

Shock is not something we graduate from in grief. It is something that we move in and out of, numerous times, as needed. Our hearts need time to grasp the enormity of what happened. Even years later, we might have trouble coming to grips with it.

We don't want this to be happening. We don't want this to be real. We want our child back. Now.

"No wonder I'm in shock. How could I not be? I love you so much."

QUESTIONS TO CONSIDER:

When and how have you experienced shock in your grief process?

Do you still experience moments of shock from time to time? What are these times like for you?

FROM A FELLOW GRIEVING PARENT:

"I still go in and out of shock. You will too. Our hearts can't accept that they're gone."

CHAPTER 2

STUNNED: "I CAN HARDLY TALK"

"There is a feeling of disbelief that comes over you, that takes over, and you kind of go through the motions."

— Frederick Barthelme

"I CAN'T THINK. I CAN hardly talk," Steve stammered, as he sat in the booth across from me.

When I entered the restaurant and sat down, Steve didn't see me. He was looking at the menu. I sat there for several minutes, unnoticed, while Steve stared at the same fixed point on the page.

When I softly cleared my throat, Steve slowly raised his head and blinked.

"Hi Gary. I didn't see you come in," he said slowly.

Everything seemed to be in slow motion for Steve.

His daughter Stephanie had been killed in a car crash a few days prior. Everything since then had been a blur, including the funeral. She was 16.

Steve and his wife Bonnie were stunned. Their lives had been forever changed in an instant.

THE UNTHINKABLE STUNS US

When death strikes, it can be merciless. The loss of a child is unthinkable. When the unthinkable becomes reality, we're stunned.

It's like being smacked on the head with a brick dropped from a 5-story building. We didn't see it coming. At first, we don't know what hit us.

We stagger, stumble, and fall. The best we can hope for is to lay there and still be able to breathe somehow.

The magnitude of the hit is so great, our minds can't begin to process it. Our hearts refuse to do so. The world just cracked in two.

We find ourselves momentarily frozen, immobile. We're awake, but not all there. We can't be. The truth would kill us instantly.

We stare. We blink. We can't think. We mumble.

Call it disbelief. Call it denial. We're stunned. We should be.

"I'm stunned. How can this be? I don't want to believe it."

QUESTIONS TO CONSIDER:

Does anything from Steve's experience resonate with you? If so, what?

Most of us are good at putting on an act. Do you give yourself permission to be "stunned?"

FROM A FELLOW GRIEVING PARENT:

"I literally couldn't talk, but I could cry. I did a lot of that. Still do. Sometimes tears are better than words anyway."

CHAPTER 3

SURREAL: "THIS IS WEIRD"

"In the midst of a world that moves, I alone am still."

— *Natsume Soseki*

"THIS IS WEIRD. EVERYTHING IS different, but it all looks the same. It's like living in some kind of alternate universe," Craig shared. "But then I walk into Matthew's room and the nightmare becomes real all over again."

Craig's son Matthew contracted spinal meningitis and died within a matter of days over the Christmas holidays. He was 13.

Like many child losses, Mathew's illness and death came out of nowhere. The shock was immense.

The shock waves soon hit Matthew's friends and class-mates. Practically the entire school was at the funeral. Most were stunned and silent. There was simply nothing to say that could make much of a difference.

"Surreal. I guess that's what you would call it. Nothing seems real," Craig concluded.

For weeks, Matthew's family lived in the stunned silence of the surreal. Matthew's absence was palpable. Everything felt weird, and wrong.

LIVING IN AN ALTERNATE UNIVERSE

When our lives are struck by loss, our world changes immediately. Of course, we don't experience all the changes at once. We experience them over the days, months, and even years that follow. This creates a "disconnect" between us and the world at large.

Our world is different. We have a new, huge hole in our hearts. So we find ourselves in this in-between place. We know our child is gone, but a part of us hasn't accepted that yet. We don't want to accept it, or perhaps we just can't.

Our world has cracked wide open, but we don't know what this fully means. We do know the whole world seems empty because our child is no longer in it.

"Everything is weird now. You're not here anymore, and I don't want that to be real."

QUESTIONS TO CONSIDER:

How have things seemed surreal to you since the loss of your child?

Do you find yourself looking at the world differently than you did before? In what way?

FROM A FELLOW GRIEVING PARENT:

"Grief will come in waves. When it comes, go with it. You will get through grief by grieving."

CHAPTER 4

SADNESS: "IT'S ALL SO SAD"

---

*"I hadn't known I was capable of being so sad,
and the discovery shocked and terrified me."*

— Hillary T. Smith

"I'M CERTAIN MY TEAR DUCTS are empty. I've been a crying fool for weeks. I've wanted to wail and scream on many occasions, but I haven't given myself permission yet," Amanda said.

Amanda's daughter Sonya died in a car crash caused by a drunk driver. Sonya left behind a husband and a baby girl. She was 26. Amanda's small community was crushed by the news.

I looked around Amanda's home. Family pictures were everywhere. Sympathy cards from friends, co-workers, and neighbors were piled on the entry table to the left. The house was dark, as if the family's light had been extinguished.

"How can she be gone? Such a wonderful, beautiful, brilliant young woman. I feel robbed," Amanda shared, putting her head in her hands. "My heart is shattered. It's all so sad...so very sad."

SADNESS IS A HUGE PART OF GRIEF

Loss is heavy. The death of a child is crushing. It

shatters hearts. Once some of the shock dissipates, a deep and abiding sadness begins to leak out.

The sadness strikes as an intense, stabbing pain. Or it can surface as a dull, chronic ache. Or both.

Our shoulders slump. We gaze down a lot. We sigh more than ever. We sit for moments, even hours, without moving, oblivious to our environment. Everything seems serious, and heavy.

Our child is no longer with us. That's sad. Terribly sad. And the sadness will pour out of us for quite some time.

Our world doesn't like sadness. Smiling faces are expected out there. What do we do? Fake it? Deny the sadness bubbling up within us? Or do we dare express it? If so, how? And when?

Sadness is one of the most common and powerful emotions in grief. Sadness is natural, and normal. Our sadness honors our child and proclaims our love.

"I'm terribly sad. That's natural. I love
you and miss you desperately."

QUESTIONS TO CONSIDER:

What about your child do you miss most right now?

At what times do memories of your child trigger feelings of sadness?

Do you feel you can express your sadness? In what ways, and with whom?

FROM A FELLOW GRIEVING PARENT:

"You will always long for your child. It will always hurt.
But the longing and the pain will change over time."

CHAPTER 5

ANGER: "I MIGHT EXPLODE!"

"So much grief, so much anger."

— *Richelle Mead*

"I MIGHT EXPLODE! I DON'T think I've ever been this angry, not even close!" Mandy said, staring out the window with her hands on her hips.

"How could this happen? Out of all the streets, why ours? Out of all the possible targets, why Lance? The total senselessness of it makes me sick," she continued.

Mandy's son Lance had been the victim of a drive-by shooting. They lived in a safe neighborhood. Lance had been a good student, and a popular one. He was 15.

"Unbelievable. Unthinkable. Unfair. Cruel. Senseless. Evil," Mandy said. "I can think of a lot of words to describe this, but none of them do it justice."

THE ANGER IS REAL

Anger can be a large component of grief, especially in the loss of a child.

We get angry at the person or people responsible — individuals we believe share some blame for what happened.

We get angry at the person or people who might have been able to prevent this.

We get angry at ourselves for not being able to protect our own children.

We get angry at God for allowing such an awful, unthinkable tragedy to take place.

We get angry at the world for being such an uncaring and cold place. How dare it blaze forward as if nothing has happened?

We get angry at the sheer backwards nature of the whole thing. Children aren't supposed to die. A parent shouldn't have to bury their child.

Our hearts tremble. When we sense our child has been taken from us, anger is a natural and common parental response.

It would seem callous not to be angry about such an injustice. It would be as if we never really loved our child.

"You've been taken from me. I'm angry about that. I miss you."

SOME THINGS TO CONSIDER:

Anger is a powerful emotion. Many of us don't know what to do when it invades our lives. How we handle it matters.

Anger is a part of the grief process for almost everyone. We must somehow allow ourselves to acknowledge the anger, and then express it in healthy ways. If we don't, it will leak out in ways we will most likely regret.

Here are ten simple ways to let the anger out, suggested by other grieving parents:

1. Buy a punching bag and some gloves, and use them regularly.

2. Exercise regularly at a moderate pace.
3. Find a quiet place by yourself to scream and yell.
4. Write out the anger either in a journal or letter.
5. Get some stress balls and squeeze them throughout the day.
6. Get a cheap set of dishes and break them one-by-one.
7. Draw or paint pictures of your anger.
8. Speed walk around, punching the air.
9. Pound a pillow.
10. Smash a dozen eggs — carefully.

What do you find yourself angry about in the loss of your child?

How have you been able to express your anger so far?

FROM A FELLOW GRIEVING PARENT:

"Lean into your grief. Let yourself feel whatever you are feeling. Don't compare your grief to anyone else's. It is yours alone."

CHAPTER 6

ANXIETY: "I'M ANXIOUS ABOUT EVERYTHING NOW"

"I think life is full of anxieties and fears and tears. It has a lot of grief in it, and it can be very grim."

— Charles M. Schultz

"WHAT'S HAPPENING TO ME?" MAUREEN asked, her voice trembling.

"I'm nervous. I shake inside. I wake up panicky in the middle of the night. I can't settle down. Yesterday, I had an anxiety attack in the grocery store," she continued. "I seem to be anxious all the time, about everything."

Maureen's daughter Molly began having sudden vision problems. A visit to the eye doctor morphed into a trip to the ER. By the end of the day, Maureen had been told that Molly had an advanced, inoperable brain tumor.

Molly died two years later. She was eight years old.

Molly's treatment was an intense, exhausting process. Those two years seemed like a lifetime. Her parents managed to hold it together through it all. Soon after the funeral, however, things changed. The intense activity came to a grinding halt, and all the anxiety stored up in them began to spurt out.

"I worry about everything. What's going to happen next? Who's next?" Maureen asked, hands shaking, her eyes pleading for relief.

ANXIETY IS COMMON IN GRIEF

When loss shatters our world, anxiety is usually one of the results.

Our sense of control is gone. We feel helpless. We wonder what will happen next.

Our child's death calls many things into question. The world and life are not as fair as we imagined. We're not as powerful as we thought. We're have far less control than we dreamed.

Anything can happen at any time to ourselves or to anyone we love and care about.

Anxiety is the natural result.

We are limited beings. We can only handle so much stress, loss, and tragedy. The anxiety builds. Sooner or later, we begin to feel it. It slowly leaks, spurts out, or bursts forth in a flood.

Our lives have been forcefully altered. Anxiety and panic attacks are common.

Anxiety is a natural expression of our grief.

"I'm anxious. That's natural. Losing you is traumatic."

AN EXERCISE TO TRY:

"Just breathe," is a common phrase in grief recovery circles. Breathing deeply can be one of the best practices to implement when anxiety hits.

Take some time now, and breathe.

- Close your eyes and breathe in deeply and slowly through your nose.

- Then let it out slowly through your mouth.

- Repeat, again and again.

- Do this for several minutes, focusing on your own breathing as much as possible.

Do this simple breathing exercise at least once each day. Practicing it when you're not anxious is important. Once deep breathing becomes a habit, you can apply it much more easily when anxiety or panic strikes.

Over time, a well-practiced habit of breathing deeply can make a huge difference.

FROM A FELLOW GRIEVING PARENT:

"The loss of a child strips you to the core, and there are times you will have to remind yourself to breathe. Breathe! You can survive. You will survive."

CHAPTER 7

FEAR: "I'M TERRIFIED"

"No one ever told me that grief felt so like fear."

— C.S. Lewis

"I'M TERRIFIED. I'M AFRAID OF everything now," Eddy said, her head in her hands.

Eddy's adult daughter Cassie had been killed in a high-speed, five-car accident, along with her husband and her two small children. She was 30.

"A whole family gone, just like that," she said, snapping her fingers.

"How do I live in a world where things like this can happen? I can barely get in a car anymore, let alone drive. I want to grab the rest of my family and lock us all in this house! I'm scared stiff. What's going to happen next? I can't afford to lose anyone else," Eddy shared.

FEAR CAN BE POWERFUL

When the loss of a child hits our lives, our world is shattered. Fear is a common and natural result.

After all, if this can happen, what else might?

The death of our child surfaces fears we didn't know we

had. Suddenly we're staring at our own mortality — along with the mortality of everyone else we love and care about.

Accidents. Sudden illnesses. Natural disasters. Diseases. Violence. Murder. War.

Anything. Any time. Anywhere. Anyone.

As C.S. Lewis said, grief can feel much like fear.

Fear and anxiety go hand-in-hand. Terror and panic often come visiting together.

Fear is a natural and common part of grieving the loss of a child.

"No wonder I'm afraid. Your death is like a nightmare."

QUESTIONS TO CONSIDER:

What fears have surfaced for you since the death of your child?

How do you typically deal with these fears?

AN EXERCISE TO TRY:

When fear strikes, taking some form of action can help unplug the fear's intensity.

Here's a simple action you can take when you find yourself afraid:

- Find a small object to symbolize your fear (it can be anything you can hold easily in one hand — a pen, pencil, keys, etc.).
- Take a moment and breathe deeply (see the exercise in the previous chapter!).
- Grip the object (your fear) tightly in your hand, and continue to breathe deeply.

- Verbalize your fear: "I'm afraid of / that..."
- Slowly release your grip on the object and let it fall.
- Continue breathing deeply.
- Ask yourself, "Is there another action I can take to unplug this fear?"

This exercise illustrates some key elements in dealing with fear:

- Acknowledge the fear.
- Identify the fear — label it as specifically as possible.
- Feel the fear, and then release it.
- If possible, take action to further unplug the fear.

FROM A FELLOW GRIEVING PARENT:

"Writing out my thoughts and feelings was the single most helpful thing I did. Be real. Be honest."

CHAPTER 8

GUILT: "IT'S MY FAULT"

"Grief is an ocean, and guilt the undertow that pulls me beneath the waves and drowns me."

— *Shaun David Hutchinson*

"THE GUILT IS EATING ME up. It's like my insides are being put through a meat grinder. The pain is unbelievable," Tanya shared.

Tanya lost three children who never took a breath. Her third, a son, was stillborn. She had always wanted a family and longed to be a mother.

"I did something wrong, somehow. The problem has to be me, right? Was it my lifestyle? Diet? Genetics? Whatever it is, it's my fault!" she stammered, weeping.

GUILT CAN BE A POWERFUL FORCE

When loss hits us, at first we're stunned, shocked. We cannot fathom our new reality. Our child is dead? How can this be?

Our hearts need to make sense out of this. Our minds search frantically for a reason for this loss. Perhaps someone, somewhere is responsible. We look for someone to blame. Often, that someone is us.

After all, we're the parent. We're supposed to protect our children. We didn't. Or we couldn't. Or we failed before we even had the chance to see them take their first breath.

If we had only...

If only we had not....

If we had known that...

Why didn't we...?

We must hit something, so we emotionally hit ourselves — over and over, and over again.

Guilt is sneaky. It is powerful and relentless. It accomplishes nothing. It is not our friend.

Guilt keeps us from living. It keeps us stuck. It hinders positive and healthy grieving.

We know this, but guilt is so familiar. We get its voice confused with our own. Beating ourselves up becomes as natural as breathing.

Guilt is a common experience for those who've lost of child. If we want to continue to love and honor our child's memory, however, we're going to have to let go of it somehow.

"What did I miss? Surely I could have done something! I feel guilty."

QUESTIONS TO CONSIDER:

As you look back at your child's death, do you feel anything was "your fault?" If so, what?

AN EXERCISE TO TRY:

Do you feel guilty? If so, try this simple exercise we used for fear in the last chapter:

- Identify what you feel guilty about. "I feel guilty about..." Be as specific as possible.

- Find an object to represent this guilt (it can be as simple as a pen or paperclip).

- Grip your "guilt" tightly in your hand.

- Begin breathing deeply and relax. Feel the object in your hand and focus on what it symbolizes.

- When you're ready, slowly release your grip and let the object fall.

- Continue breathing deeply.

Guilt is common in the loss of a child, but it is not our friend. Letting go of it and forgiving ourselves can be challenging. We'll talk more about this in a later chapter.

FROM A FELLOW GRIEVING PARENT:

"Guilt is huge. Don't go there. If you allow it entrance, it will block every forward step you attempt."

CHAPTER 9

BITTER: "I FEEL POISONED"

"The fairest things have fleetest end,
Their scent survives their close:
But the rose's scent is bitterness
To her who loved the rose."

— *Francis Thompson*

"I DON'T SAY MUCH ANYMORE. I'm too bitter. I'm afraid of what will come out," Wes said.

Wes hadn't said much since his son Cole died. Cole was a smart, good-looking, well-liked athlete. Late one night, the driver of the car Cole and his buddies were in lost control and veered off the road. The car flipped and took out two trees. Only the driver survived, and he walked away almost without a scratch. Cole was 15.

"I started out mad, and it went downhill from there. I went internal, and stayed there. I feel poisoned, and like everything I do or say is laced with it," Wes shared.

PAIN CAN PRODUCE BITTERNESS

When a child dies, dreams go up in smoke. Long-held expectations are shattered. The future we planned on is gone.

Part of us died with our child. We're shocked, stunned.

31

We get sad, and angry. In some cases, the anger in us festers and spreads. We grow bitter.

Like anger, bitterness leaks. Similar to a slow but raging infection, it seeps into our souls and then pours out of our hearts and into our lives — and onto the lives of those around us. Losing a child is such a tragedy, such an unexpected shock that any of us can easily wind up here. Unexpressed, unresolved anger can give birth to a reservoir of bitterness, perhaps without us even realizing it.

Bitterness is not unusual in cases of child loss, but it is not healthy or helpful. The loss of a child is hard enough without being complicated by this internal, cold, festering rage. Bitterness can dupe us into indulging deeper in its poisons, causing us to pile up regrets that confuse and complicate our grief.

We can love our children by dealing responsibly with bitterness when we discover its presence. We can honor their lives and memory by learning to let go of this festering poison.

There is an old saying: "If the root is bitter, so will the fruit be." Cleaning our roots can help us survive the loss of our child.

"Bitterness is easy to indulge in. Instead, I'll choose to remember you by loving."

QUESTIONS TO CONSIDER:

Have you seen or sensed bitterness growing in your heart? How so?

What do you think it would look like, for the sake of your child, for you to let go of that bitterness?

SOME POSSIBLE ACTION STEPS:

If you're aware of bitterness forming in your heart, now is the time to begin to deal with it. Here are some possible action steps:

- Consider doing the exercise from the last chapter. Identify specifically what you're bitter about and go through the process of beginning to release it.

- Talk to someone safe that you trust (we'll discuss "safe people" in chapter 39). Tell them you're feeling bitter and that you need to vent.

- Go to a support group. Listen to the stories of others. When you're ready, share that you're growing bitter. Begin to get it out.

- Reach out to a grief counselor (try local hospices or grief centers) or therapist.

Like venom from a rattlesnake bite, the important thing is getting the poison out in healthy ways. Don't let bitterness take over your heart. You're too important and valuable. Take one of the above action steps today.

FROM A FELLOW GRIEVING PARENT:

"I nearly destroyed myself. I was so bitter. Please forgive, and forgive quickly. This honors your child more than you know."

CHAPTER 10

NUMB: "I'M NOT SURE I FEEL ANYTHING"

*"To me, grief is a devastating numbness,
every sensation dulled."*

— *Veronica Roth*

"I'M JUST HERE. I GO through the motions. People ask me how I'm doing. I shrug my shoulders. I don't know. You tell me. How should I be doing?" Todd asked.

Todd's son Toby grew up wanting to be a soldier. He enlisted in the Marines right out of high school. He served three tours of duty. The trauma of battle stayed with him. After a year of trying to readjust back home, Toby took his own life. He was 29.

"How do I feel? I'm not sure I feel anything. I'm numb," Todd said.

WE CAN GROW NUMB

Our hearts have been shattered. We lay in pieces, all over the floor. Like Humpty-Dumpty, we know that no one and nothing can put us back together the way we were. It's impossible. Part of us is missing now.

We experience shock, sadness, anger, fear, anxiety, and

much more. Emotions swirl around and batter us incessantly. It's overwhelming. After a while, we can cease to feel. We grow numb.

In the medical and dental world, we're numbed and anesthetized so we don't feel the excruciating, perhaps unbearable pain that surgery brings. We're protected from the full force of what's happening at the time. And that's a good thing.

Numbness is designed to be temporary. As time goes on, the anesthesia wears off, and we begin to feel some of the pain of the trauma that took place.

Numbness in grief is also ideally a temporary rest stop—an impermanent protective shield against the full emotional-mental-physical-spiritual force of our loss. This numbed-out place is not meant to be a new residence for us. It cannot sustain our hearts, our relationships, and our purpose in life.

But if the pain is intense enough, and if there are enough complicating factors involved (violence, family dynamics, criminal circumstances, not getting to say goodbye, etc.), our hearts can slip into semi-permanent hiding. Our internal "feelers" can shut down. Numb can become a way of life.

Numbness is common in grief, in temporary stages. This protects our hearts when we need it. We will come out of it in time.

"My heart is so bruised, sometimes I feel nothing. I miss you."

QUESTIONS TO CONSIDER:

Have you experienced some emotional numbness since your child died? What was this like?

What has been helpful to you (people, events, groups, activities) when numb?

SOME POSSIBLE ACTION STEPS:

If you've been numb for a while and you sense this state is more than just temporary, please consider doing one or all of the following:

- Reach out to your medical doctor. Share with them and get their input.

- Contact a grief counselor (check local hospices, grief centers, or hospitals) or a therapist. We could all benefit from professional grief help.

- Talk to someone you trust and share your situation. Ask them to check in with you regularly (set a time period — daily, weekly, etc.). Or you can be the initiator and touch base with them.

FROM A FELLOW GRIEVING PARENT:

"I go in and out of being numb, but I stay there less and less. It's okay to be where you are, but try not to get stuck there."

CHAPTER 11

LOST: "I FEEL LIKE A SHADOW"

"Lost opportunities, lost possibilities, feelings we can never get back. That's part of what it means to be alive."

— *Haruki Murakami*

"I FEEL LIKE A SHADOW. I'm a fraction of my former self. The days go by, and I hardly notice them. Everything is a foggy blur," Wendy shared.

Wendy's son Luke was born with cerebral palsy. Wendy vowed early that she would give him the best childhood possible. Luke did well. He was friendly and engaging. He loved people and animals. The sheer weight of caregiving wore Wendy down, but she delighted in it at the same time.

Pneumonia cut Luke's life short at 15. Wendy was devastated. Not only had she lost her son and only child, but she felt cut adrift and purposeless.

"Luke was my life. Who am I now? I'm lost," she said.

WE CAN FEEL LOST

We can feel lost when our child dies. This is natural and common. So much of our lives were wrapped up in them, whether they were minors or adults.

We knew them all their lives (unless of course, we adopted them later). We watched them grow, learn, and mature. We delighted as they moved from stage to stage. We met their joys, obstacles, and pains with them.

Our lives become so intertwined, so connected, that it can become difficult to separate ourselves from them—especially emotionally. Parenting is thrilling, scary, challenging, hard, fun, and exhausting. If our child had disabilities or special challenges, extra forms of caregiving get added into the mix.

No matter who they are, however, we instinctively know that our kids are vulnerable. We provide for and protect them. We nurture hopes and dreams for them.

So much of our lives revolve around our kids that whenever one of them exits, at whatever age, they leave a huge, gaping hole in our existence.

Who are we now? Why are we here? What's next? These are important questions.

No wonder we can feel lost.

"I love you so much. I feel lost without you."

QUESTIONS TO CONSIDER:

Feeling lost can come from a sense of total separation from your child. Part of grieving is keeping them alive in your heart. They are a part of you, and staying connected to them somehow is important.

Picture your child for a moment. What are some of the things you miss most?

Think of a fun, delightful time you enjoyed with your child. Talk about it out loud, or write about it.

SOME POSSIBLE ACTION STEPS:

If you're feeling lost or purposeless in your grief, you might want to consider one or some of the following:

- Give your grief purpose by volunteering or serving in honor of your child.

- Check out a support group (local hospice, The Compassionate Friends, Bereaved Parents, church groups, etc.). Being with others also enduring grief can be hope-giving and encouraging in many different ways.

- Write down stories and memories. Write letters to your child. Compose a "list poem" of all the things you cherish and miss about them. Write in a journal, specifically about feeling lost. Writing can help us process what's happening inside us.

- Ask someone you trust if they would be willing to listen while you talk about your child. For most of us, the more we share, the less lost we feel.

Talk. Share. Write. Tell your story.

FROM A FELLOW GRIEVING PARENT:

"Take one moment, even one second at a time. Don't expect too much of yourself too soon. This is a long, tough process."

CHAPTER 12

DEPRESSED: "THE COLOR IS GONE"

"I saw the world in black and white instead of the vibrant colours and shades I knew existed."

— *Katie McGarry*

"I EAT. HE DRINKS. I talk. He doesn't. We both go through the motions, trying to somehow be strong for our other kids. Every day is an uphill battle," Mandy shared.

Mandy and Mike's son Marcus had been looking forward to college for years. He was a serious student, who also loved to party. When he arrived on campus, one of the first things he did was attend rush. He became a pledge in a prestigious fraternity.

One night, the alcohol was flowing and Marcus kept drinking—much more than usual. In the middle of the night, his roommate found him on the bathroom floor. Marcus never regained consciousness. He was 19.

"The color is gone. I have no spark, no interest. I don't want to go anywhere, see anyone, or do anything. It's like a heavy, wet blanket is smothering all of us," Mandy said. "I'm depressed. We're all depressed."

THE LOSS OF A CHILD IS DEPRESSING

Experiencing some depression in grief is natural and common. We've lost a child. Their absence has left a gaping hole in our hearts. It feels wrong to have joy in anything.

As Mandy said, the color goes out of life. We wonder if it will ever return, or if it even can.

Our eating and sleeping habits take a hit. We're fatigued all the time. We walk around in a fog, sometimes forgetting where we're going and why. We wonder incessantly about questions we'll probably never know the answers to. We slip back or deeper into unhealthy habits or addictions.

We withdraw from the world and people. We feel alone, no matter where we are or who we're around. We're starved for fun, but feel terribly guilty about having any.

We slog through each day like we're knee-deep in mud. Motivation has disappeared. Even brushing our teeth is an emotional chore. We sigh a lot.

With all of this, plus the daily, relentless assault of unpredictable emotions, it isn't surprising that symptoms of depression can overtake us for a period of time.

"Life without you is depressing. No wonder I feel this way."

QUESTIONS TO CONSIDER:

What elements of depression have you seen in yourself so far? (Changes in eating or sleeping habits, motivation, energy, mood, relationships, withdrawal, disinterest in life, addiction issues, fierce denial, hopelessness, etc.)

SOME POSSIBLE ACTION STEPS:

Most depression is temporary. It comes, and it goes. We experience it for periods of time, from hours to days, or perhaps a week. When this temporary depression strikes, consider one of the following:

- Intentionally get out among people (a movie, restaurant, play, the mall, church, etc.).

- Volunteer to serve in honor of your child (church, food bank, civic organization, health organization, etc.).

- Talk to someone you trust (friend, therapist, mentor, minister, grief counselor) about how you're feeling. Talking about it can make a big difference.

- Write it out. Journals. Letters. Whatever it takes. Try to capture how you're doing and feeling on paper. This helps express our emotions and process our grief.

- What creative activity did you enjoy earlier in your life (drawing, painting, crafting, woodworking, etc.)? Do some of that. Creative expression aids in healing.

If the depression you're experiencing has deepened and become your new lifestyle, you need to take action now.

If you are experiencing the following...

- You don't get out of bed.
- You isolate yourself from other people and activities.
- You fall deeply into an addiction or self-medicating behavior

- You are non-functional when it comes to daily routine life.

- You have thoughts of harming yourself.

...please call your physician, a mental health professional, or 911 immediately.

FROM A FELLOW GRIEVING PARENT:

"Grieve. Don't hold anything in. He or she was your child. They are worth it!"

WHERE WE'VE BEEN AND WHERE WE'RE GOING:

The loss of a child can have devastating emotional impact.

We're shocked and stunned. We're sad, angry, and anxious. We can be hit with depression, panic, and confusion. Everything seems surreal.

We can feel lost and alone. Sometimes we feel nothing at all.

This complicated and often unpredictable mix of emotion is common and natural for parents enduring this nightmare. In this section, we've discussed the scope of this emotional tsunami and how to survive it in a sane and healthy way.

The death of child not only impacts us emotionally, but mentally as well. Our minds, as well as our hearts, will feel the shock. We'll talk more about this in the next section.

PART TWO:

The Mental Impact

WHEN DEATH STRIKES, IT KNOCKS us senseless. We're stunned and reeling, gasping for air, wondering what hit us. Our hearts are shattered. Emotions leak all over the place.

While riding this emotional roller-coaster, we soon find that our minds are not what they used to be. We're often confused and frustrated. We forget things and have trouble focusing. We can have memory gaps, and space out at times. Our minds spin from the constant, relentless assault of unanswerable questions.

The mental and emotional stress can drive us to old (or new) negative behavior patterns or addictions. We wonder about our sanity at times. Some have suicidal thoughts.

The death of a child is a mind-bending experience. How do we survive this?

In this section, we'll discuss the powerful impact the loss of a child can have on us mentally. We'll talk about the natural and common cognitive effects that most grieving parents experience and how to handle them in a healthy and responsible way.

Breathe deeply. You might feel like you're going crazy, but chances are you're not. Read on and see...

CHAPTER 13

CONFUSION: "I DON'T KNOW WHICH END IS UP"

---

*"For in grief nothing 'stays put.' One keeps on
emerging from a phase, but it always recurs.
Round and round. Everything repeats. Am I going
in circles, or dare I hope I am on a spiral?
But if a spiral, am I going up or down it?"*

-C.S. Lewis

"I DON'T KNOW WHICH END is up. I'm so confused," Donna said.

Donna's daughter Lacey was an elementary school teacher who was making a difference. Lacey had a supportive husband and two little girls. She was enjoying her life, family, and career, until sudden severe headaches revealed multiple lesions in her brain. Lacey died within a year. She was 31.

"It happened so fast. On the other hand, it seemed like everything was in slow motion. We couldn't get enough time. Now, I wake up in the middle of the night, my thoughts racing. My mind is all over the place. Did that really happen? No, it couldn't have. Not Lacey. She can't be gone. I need to call her," Donna continued.

"It's like I experience her death over and over again, multiple times every day."

LOSS IS CONFUSING

Experiencing some mental confusion in grief is natural and common. Loss hits us on all fronts. The death of a child is confusing.

We're confused about how such a thing could happen. Surely it didn't have to be this way. Certainly someone somewhere could have done something at some time to stop this from happening.

We're confused about what to think and how to feel. We're confused about who we are now and how to live life. How do we live on when our child is dead?

We're confused about all the changes that are occurring. The losses keep piling up. We bump into another source of pain with every step. Our child is gone, and this changes everything.

We're confused about other people and our relationships. Some people we counted on have disappeared. Others act weird and tentative around us, like our grief is some kind of contagious disease.

We're confused about how to deal with all this in a healthy way — including how to be there for our other kids and family members. How can we care for others when we're barely able to get out of bed? How do we support others who are grieving when our shattered hearts are in pieces strewn all over the place?

We're confused about the future. How do we think about that? The future we expected and hoped for is gone. Whatever dreams we had have been either crushed or mangled beyond recognition.

The world as we knew it is no longer.

Yes, this is confusing.

"No wonder I'm confused. Life without you is unimaginable."

QUESTIONS TO CONSIDER:

Since your child's death, what have you found yourself confused about? Consider making a list.

From your list above, which have been the most difficult for you?

Which item on your list are you struggling with the most right now?

Can you think of a healthy action step you can take in dealing with this issue (i.e. talking to a safe person, a support group, writing, serving, etc.)?

FROM A FELLOW GRIEVING PARENT:

"Confusion is part of this, and some things will never make sense. This is hard for me to swallow, but I'm getting there."

CHAPTER 14

CRAZY: "I Feel Unhinged at Times"

"The pain of the leaving can tear us apart."

— Henri Nouwen

"MY EMOTIONS ARE ERRATIC. My mind either churns or completely shuts down. I can't rest. I'm always on the verge of tears," Claudia shared.

Claudia's daughter Ashleigh was born premature. It had been a difficult pregnancy, and Ashleigh came out of the womb with a host of issues. Over the next 6 weeks, she had multiple surgeries and procedures, to no avail. Ashleigh never left the hospital.

"I know she suffered. The thought of that drives me nuts. I feel unhinged, like I'm coming apart. I feel trapped. Sometimes I can't breathe," Claudia said.

Claudia looked down for a moment before continuing. "Maybe I'm going crazy," she concluded.

LOSS CAN MAKE US QUESTION OUR SANITY

Most people feel crazy at some point (or at several points) in their grief process. Feeling like we might be losing it is natural and common for grieving hearts.

Our emotions resemble a poorly-constructed, out-of-control, and somewhat dangerous roller-coaster. Emotions unpredictably climb, fall, twist, turn, and drop. We don't feel anything like ourselves.

Our bodies betray us. Strange come-and-go symptoms assault us. Stress pounds our physical health. We feel like we're falling apart.

Our minds spin. Racing thoughts are common. We forget things. We can't concentrate. We feel like a shadow of our former selves. What's happening to us?

Like Claudia, we can feel unhinged at times, similar to being on the edge of a cliff or on top of a deep, could-give-way-at-any-moment sinkhole.

Bereavement researchers refer to this as the "Going Crazy Syndrome." It feels like we're going nuts. The truth is, however, that we feel crazy because we're in a crazy situation.

If we're immersed in craziness, we're going to be impacted by that. We tend to personalize things and think that the "crazy" is coming from us.

Our child has died. That's crazy. We're in the center of this, and it will make us think we're nuts at times too.

"Life without you is nuts. Yes, I feel crazy sometimes."

A QUESTION TO CONSIDER:

Have you felt a little crazy since the death of your child? How so?

POSSIBLE ACTION STEPS:

Feeling looney or unhinged is no fun. Here are some possible action steps to help:

- Continue to develop the habit of breathing deeply (see the exercise in chapter 6 for more information). Again, this is a simple but powerful skill that can make a big difference.

- Find a grief support group (Bereaved Parents, Compassionate Friends, local hospices, grief centers, churches, etc.). Being with other people who are experiencing their own version of "grief craziness" can be affirming and relieving.

- Reach out to a grief counselor, therapist, or minister. Sometimes reassurance and feedback from a professional can help immensely.

Feeling crazy? Chances are it's not you. It's grief.

FROM A FELLOW GRIEVING PARENT:

"I felt crazy. Losing a child will do that to you. Feeling a little nuts becomes normal."

CHAPTER 15

RACING THOUGHTS: "MY MIND SPINS"

"Everyone can master a grief but he that has it."

— *William Shakespeare*

"I CAN'T SIT STILL. WHEN I try, my insides quiver. My mind is like a room full of superballs, bouncing randomly in all directions. Sometimes, my head hurts with all the activity," Brad said.

Brad's son Barron contracted AIDS, most likely from a dirty needle. His family went into shock at the news, and then into panic. Ten years of treatment slowed the disease process, but Barron finally succumbed to a variety of infections. He was 37.

"I watched him suffer, dwindle, and slowly fade away. I knew this was coming. I've been preparing myself for a decade. But no amount of time, energy, or study could have prepared me for his final breath. No wonder my head hurts," Brad shared.

OUR MINDS SPIN

When loss hits, it affects us mentally. Our brains struggle to make sense of it all. Our minds shift into overdrive. Racing thoughts are natural and common for those of us who are grieving.

Our brains search incessantly for answers. Why did this happen? How? Could it have been avoided? What could I, we, or anyone have done differently that would have made a difference? Who's responsible for this?

Certain images are burned into our consciousness, especially if we witnessed trauma to our child, or their death or decline. Nightmares invade. Sleep is disturbed, or flees altogether. Some of us may even be afraid to close our eyes. We've seen enough. We don't want to see anymore.

Our thoughts spin, with little to no resolution, like some continuously revolving door that does nothing except circulate a little air. We want off this mental merry-go-around, but how?

Some of us need medication to slow down this mental runaway train enough to be functional in daily life. There is no shame in this. All of us need assistance from a variety of sources and people if we're going to make it through this halfway intact.

Some medicate in other ways, attempting to quiet these raging thoughts with alcohol, drugs, sex, food, or shopping. Anything for some relief. This solves nothing, however, and the racing thoughts return with a vengeance if not processed in a healthy manner.

Our minds spin. Racing thoughts are natural and common. Losing a child is a mentally shaking experience.

"My mind is never still. I'm always thinking about and looking for you."

AN EXERCISE TO TRY:

Racing thoughts can be frustrating. Here are three simple things you can try — Breathe, Write, Talk.

- **Breathe:** Making deep breathing a practiced habit can be a huge weapon in your arsenal when attacked by racing thoughts. Take some time each day and practice breathing (check chapter 6 for details). Then apply this when you have racing thoughts.

- **Write:** Prepare some paper, a spiral notebook, or a journal. When your mind spins, grab a pen or pencil and write down what you're thinking (no matter how weird or ridiculous some of it is). The act of writing slows down your mind and forces you to focus. As you write, you will usually notice yourself growing calmer.

- **Talk:** Get by yourself and begin to speak your thoughts out loud. Yes, talk to yourself. Simply say what you're thinking as you are thinking it. This too slows your mind down, as your brain works to put thoughts into words. "Talking out loud" can be a quick, easy, and effective way to deal with racing thoughts.

What does your mind tend to race about? Are there any particular recurring themes?

Racing thoughts are natural and common in child loss. Breathe. Write. Talk.

FROM A FELLOW GRIEVING PARENT:

"Slow down. Write it out. Something happens when we do that."

CHAPTER 16

FORGETFULNESS: "I FORGET STUFF AND LOSE THINGS"

"Grief is the proof love is still here."

— *Tessa Shaffer*

"I WONDER ABOUT MY BRAIN. I forget stuff and lose things. My memory is suddenly terrible. Am I just on grief overload?" Lisa asked.

Lisa's son Nick loved football. He was the starting quarterback in high school as a sophomore. Halfway through the season, he began having dizzy spells. One day in practice, he collapsed.

Nick never regained consciousness. A rare, undetected heart condition took his life. He was 16.

"I'll never see him graduate, fall in love, or get married," she said, staring at the trophies on Nick's desk. "We have two other teens, but the house feels empty. So does my brain. Some days I totally zone out. Yesterday, I honestly could not remember my own name."

WE TEND TO FORGET THINGS NOW

Grief takes up enormous space and energy. As a result, we

simply have less brain available for everyday life. This is not a permanent condition. Forgetfulness is a temporary and common grief reaction.

With less mental space available, we forget things, appointments, and why we came into the room. And of course, we can never seem to find our keys.

We may experience memory gaps about the past as well. We can't recall what we did for Thanksgiving or what we had for breakfast. Other memories get garbled, as we mix two recollections together to create one that, well, never happened (at least not the way we remember it).

If we had memory issues before, chances are grief has exacerbated them. Even people with normally perfect recall can discover things slipping through the cracks created by loss.

Forgetfulness is common and natural during times of grief. Especially when the loss is a child.

"It's amazing I remember anything.
All I can think about is you."

A QUESTION TO CONSIDER:

Have you noticed some forgetfulness invading your life since your child died? How so?

AN EXERCISE TO TRY:

Grief is tough. Some forgetfulness is common and natural. Here are some possible action steps that can help:

- Go easy on yourself. You have less brainpower available right now.

- Downgrade your expectations. It is not business or life as usual. Far from it. To expect yourself to keep the same schedule, perform at the same level, and do all you did before is unrealistic and unhealthy.

- Try making a simple list each morning (or each evening before bed). Put down 3 (and only 3) things that are your priorities for the day. Focus on these things. If you get other things done, that's bonus. And don't forget to put some self-care on your list (exercise, nutrition, rest, etc.). Taking care of yourself needs to be high on the priority list.

Forgetfulness is usually not a permanent condition. It's a common, natural, and temporary reaction to the loss of your child.

FROM A FELLOW GRIEVING PARENT:

"I couldn't remember anything. Our minds are not the same. Nothing is the same. Breathe deeply. You will bounce back, slowly."

CHAPTER 17

CONCENTRATION: "I CAN'T SEEM TO FOCUS"

"I feel so much I can't seem to think."

— *Unknown*

"I CAN'T SEEM TO FOCUS. My concentration is gone," Wayne shared. "I space out at work. I zone out in conversations. I watch movies and discover I have no idea what the plot line is."

Wayne's daughter Tory was his little princess. She was a daddy's girl, and the two of them adored each other. When she went to college, she called her dad almost every day.

Her senior year, Tory was celebrating Spring Break at a lake house with some friends. A freak boating accident ended her life. She was 18.

"I'll never forget that call. I've been living in a fog ever since. I miss my baby girl," Wayne concluded, turning to look out the window.

WE'RE NOT AS SHARP

As we discussed in the last chapter, grief takes up a large amount of mental and emotional space. It's exhausting and consumes tremendous amounts of energy. Our ability to concentrate is going to take a hit. This is natural and common.

We zone out in the middle of conversations. One moment we're engaged and the next we have no idea what's happening. We find ourselves staring into space at work. Time passes unnoticed. It's as if our systems are saying, "We're officially overloaded. We're shutting down now to prevent total meltdown."

Like a car running on fumes, we try to do life on a lot less than before. This only adds to our frustration and exhaustion. Enjoyment has gone out the window. Our attention span is reduced to seconds. Focusing becomes a task of herculean proportions.

Work, relationships, hobbies, and service can all suffer. The loss of our child is taking up enormous space in our lives, as it should. Spurts of focus are probably doable. Intense, productive concentration, however, may be unrealistic for a while.

This can't-concentrate-or-focus struggle is not permanent. Though frustrating, it is a temporary, natural, and common grief reaction.

"I can't focus or concentrate. I'm not surprised. My heart is missing you."

A QUESTION TO CONSIDER:

Have you noticed a decreased ability to concentrate since the death of your child? How so?

SOME SUGGESTIONS:

When we can't perform or focus as usual, we can grow

frustrated and angry. Here are some action steps that might help:

- Be kind to yourself. Reduced concentration and focus is normal and expected. Learning to accept yourself with this new, temporary handicap is important.

- Downgrade your expectations. Life and work are not business as usual, no matter what anyone else says or implies. You're simply not all there. You can't be. You're grieving. Adjust your expectations of yourself accordingly.

- Plan your concentration in spurts. You have smaller time windows of concentration to work with, so use them wisely. Get the most important stuff done first.

- Rest. Give yourself space. Stare at the walls. Your mind and heart need to recover from this severe trauma. Make rest a priority.

Most concentration and focus issues are temporary. Be patient with yourself. You've lost a child.

FROM A FELLOW GRIEVING PARENT:

"No parent should ever have to be a part of this club. Take it minute by minute. Do the best you can. Be merciful with yourself."

CHAPTER 18

ADDICTIONS: "I'M RUNNING, PURE AND SIMPLE."

*"There are things that happen in a person's life
that are so scorched in the memory and burned into
the heart that there's no forgetting them."*

— *John Boyne*

"I'M RUNNING, PURE AND SIMPLE," Bart said. "I was never good enough. When Tad died, I knew it was my fault somehow. I fell back into all the old stuff so easily."

Bart's son Tad was a lively, active kid. He was into everything as soon as his little legs and arms could take him there. He grew like a weed into a strong, locomotive of a toddler.

One day, Tad blitzed out into the street after a ball before Bart or his wife Kathy could get to him. Tad never saw the car coming. He died instantly. He was four.

"I was so angry. I screamed at myself. I called myself every hateful name I could think of. The mental picture of my Tad lying in the street was too much. I hit the bottle again, and I hit it hard," Bart said.

LOSS CAN TRIGGER OLD BEHAVIOR PATTERNS

Loss is painful. The death of a child is excruciating. If we try to flee from the pain, we must run to something or someone.

We might self-medicate. If we have a history of this, we're even more susceptible.

Alcohol. Drugs (illicit or prescription). Sex. Gambling. Food (eating disorders). Shopping. Activity. Work. Entertainment. Almost anything can become an addiction to attempt to numb the pain. We believe we're responsible somehow, so we punish ourselves.

Loss can trigger a cascade of self-hatred from a background of addiction, abuse, deprivation, or other heavy losses. Like a dam breaking over a quiet country village, the devastation wrought can be quick and heavy.

Child loss rattles the most stable of hearts. None of us is immune to seeking refuge in substances or activities that promise but can't possibly deliver. This death is a monstrous, traumatic, heart-shattering event. Slipping back into a familiar addiction or finding a new one can be a strong temptation.

When we go this direction, however, we inflict even more suffering — on ourselves, those we love, our other relationships, and our careers. These are deep waters. None of us can or should make this journey through grief alone. We need each other, desperately.

Our hearts hunger for comfort, peace, perspective, and hope. If we focus on grieving in healthy ways, we can provide some of this for each other.

"I'm tempted to run, but that would mean running from you. No thanks."

A QUESTION AND SOME
SUGGESTIONS TO CONSIDER:

Have you slipped into an addiction or find yourself leaning toward one after the death of your child? How so?

Any of us are susceptible to slipping into a new or old addiction at any time. If this is happening with you, please consider these important action steps:

- Find an addiction support group (AA, NA, SA, OA, GA, Celebrate Recovery, etc.) and begin attending. Don't try to do this on your own. You won't be able to.

- Find a grief support group (hospices, grief centers, churches, The Compassionate Friends, Bereaved Parents). Being with others who are grieving can be affirming and encouraging.

- Reach out for professional help (grief counselor, therapist, minister, medical doctor, etc.). All of us can benefit from involving specialists in our grief process.

Grief is a process, and so is recovery. You may feel alone, but you never are. Help is out there.

FROM A FELLOW GRIEVING PARENT:

"Don't rush through this, but don't stay stuck either. Get the help you need."

CHAPTER 19

SUICIDAL THOUGHTS:
"I WANT TO DIE TOO"

"You think you have a memory; but it has you!"

— *John Irving*

"I CAN'T LIVE WITHOUT MY son. There is no hope for me here. I need to go and be with him. I want to die too," Candy said, pleading.

Candy's son Austin was a quiet, sensitive kid. He was shy and never had many friends. Multiple moves didn't help his sense of stability and security.

Austin loved video games. Over time, the games he played turned dark, and death was a prevalent theme. Increasingly isolated, lonely, and morose, Austin took his own life. He was 16.

"I didn't see the signs. I didn't save him. It's all my fault," Candy shared, weeping profusely. "He was my life. There is nothing for me here now. Nothing."

SELF-DESTRUCTIVE THOUGHTS

In some cases, we as parents can travel down dark roads in our grief. Suicidal thoughts are one example of this.

Though such thoughts are not necessarily natural in the mourning process, they are not uncommon.

To say that we miss our child is a gross understatement. We see our child as a part of us (adopted kids too). But sometimes we can go too far. We are not our child, and they are not us.

There are times when what we think of as love can silently morph into something else — dependency, control, and enmeshment. We cease to see where we end and where our child begins. For the hearts involved, it can be difficult to discern where genuine love stops and enmeshment begins.

Instead of our child being a crucial part of our lives, they can become our life, our meaning, and our purpose on this planet. We begin to live through them. We lose ourselves in the process.

So when our child dies, it's as if we die too. They were our life and now our life is over. We are dead, with no meaning, purpose, or hope. All we can think about is being with them, no matter what that means or what it takes. We have lost any sense of self outside of them, or perhaps we have never had much of a sense of personal identity in life.

In march the suicidal thoughts, just like they belong. If we don't admit, voice, and deal with them, these self-destructive invaders can set up shop in our hearts. Thoughts that take up residence deep within us can sometimes lead to action. If this happens, one tragedy gets added to another.

"Seems like" is an important and powerful phrase in grief. It "seems like" there is no hope or that the pain is too great. But perception is not the same as truth. However, perception is reality for the person involved.

The loss of a child can fixate us on death instead of on

life. Grieving is the process of learning to adjust, over time, to this unthinkable loss in the healthiest way possible.

Though we can't see it, there is always hope. As we process our grief in responsible and healthy ways, it will show itself.

"I love you, so I will live on and honor your memory."

IF THIS APPLIES TO YOU, TAKE ACTION NOW:

Have you had, or are you having, suicidal thoughts since the death of your child? If so, take at least one of these action steps immediately:

- Call 911 or a suicide hotline.

- Reach out to someone you trust, preferably a professional (grief counselor, social worker, therapist, minister). Make the contact. Express what you're thinking. Be honest.

- If you can't do either of the above, call a good friend or someone you trust to take action on your behalf.

Don't play around with suicidal thoughts. Admit them, voice them, and deal with them by reaching out and involving others. Do this for your own sake and for the sake of all those around you.

FROM A FELLOW GRIEVING PARENT:

"Your child would want you to live. Live!
Survive! If you don't, that's one less voice to
speak their name and tell their story."

WHERE WE'VE BEEN AND WHERE WE'RE GOING...

The death of a child pounds our hearts and our minds. While we're enduring the roller-coaster emotions involved, we're also deeply affected mentally.

In this section, we discussed some of what grieving parents commonly experience. We're confused and frustrated. We can have memory gaps and trouble concentrating. Tough, often unanswerable questions assault us. Our minds spin. If we're not careful, we can easily slip back into patterns of self-destructive behavior and addictions.

We've brought these things into the open, and talked about how to begin to deal with them. We've processed some of these with specific questions to consider and exercises to try. This is tough. We need to take our wounded hearts seriously.

In addition to the heavy emotional and mental impact, the death of a child affects us physically as well. Our bodies are a big part of the grief equation. We'll talk about this in the next section.

PART THREE:

The Physical Impact

THE LOSS OF A CHILD shatters the heart and rattles the mind. In the previous two sections, we discussed the scope of the emotional and mental impact grieving parents can experience. In this section, we'll look at the affect our child's death and the resulting grief process can have on our bodies.

Many experience physical distress during grief: headaches, stomach pain, dizziness, palpitations, rapid heartbeat, numbness, exhaustion, clumsiness, frequent colds and minor illnesses, etc. Our usual eating and sleep patterns can be disrupted. Some of us might think we're falling apart.

What's happening to us?

How do we handle this?

Read on...

CHAPTER 20

PHYSICAL SYMPTOMS: "MY BODY IS FALLING APART"

"Now I know that grief is a whetstone that sharpens all your love, all your happiest memories, into blades that tear you apart from within."

— *Claudia Gray*

"I HAVE HEADACHES. MY BACK hurts. My stomach bothers me almost every day. I have dizzy spells. I think my body is falling apart," Shirley shared.

Seemingly out of the blue, Shirley's daughter Corinne was diagnosed with advanced breast cancer. The treatment was severe enough that Corrine finally opted to go on hospice care. After six months with a good quality of life, Corinne died at home surrounded by her husband, her two daughters, and the rest of her loving family. She was 44.

"After Corinne's death, I've been getting hit with one thing after another. I had tests done. Nothing. Then I wondered, could this be grief?" Shirley asked.

WHEN GRIEF GETS PHYSICAL

Many people experience new, exacerbated, or strange

physical symptoms following the death of a child. When grief hits, it smacks our bodies too.

Grief is a form of stress. As such, it naturally taxes our immune system and causes our bodies to work harder to maintain health. In the short term, we might be able to manage without too much distress. Over the long haul, however, grief can wear us down. All kinds of health issues can surface.

We can experience headaches, muscle aches, tightness in the chest, and neck pain. Some report chest pain, palpitations, or rapid heartbeat. Others complain of stomach pain, intestinal distress, bowel changes, heartburn, or nausea. Many experience air hunger (the feeling of not being able to get enough air), frequent colds, or persistent respiratory infections. The list goes on and on.

Our immune systems are suppressed. Our bodies are feeling our distress. We are more vulnerable physically.

Grief is not an illness like the common cold, where we can expect to recover and be as good as new in a few days. Grief is more like an extended battle or a demanding marathon. We must learn to pace ourselves and appreciate that our entire system is under duress.

Weathering this physically challenging storm is a long-term adventure. Taking ourselves and our bodies seriously is a key to grieving in a healing and healthy way.

The death of a child affects our whole person. Experiencing some grief-related physical symptoms is natural and common.

"I miss you so much it hurts, literally. Grief racks me, body and soul."

QUESTIONS TO CONSIDER:

Have you noticed any health changes (new, strange, or exacerbated symptoms) since the death of your child? If so, please describe them.

What are some things you might do to take your body more seriously during this time?

SOME OBVIOUS BUT IMPORTANT REMINDERS:

These almost go without saying, but making sure the following three things are in place in your life can make a radical difference in your ability to weather the grieving process well.

- Good nutrition (eating healthy and hydrating well)

- Adequate sleep (since grief is exhausting, you might need more than usual)

- Regular exercise (burns off emotion, releases endorphins, and bolsters the immune system)

Taking good care of yourself is one powerful way to love your child and honor his or her memory.

FROM A FELLOW GRIEVING PARENT:

"Grief is like an earthquake. I have bruises,
scratches, and some deeper wounds. I didn't escape
physically. Take your health seriously."

CHAPTER 21

SLEEP DISTURBANCES:
"Sleep? What's That?"

---

*"And even in sleep I was not completely free.
So often sleep brought dreams of him."*

— Bernard Taylor

"Sleep? What's that?" Paul said. "I manage to snatch a little here and there, but I haven't slept through the night since Colton died."

Paul's son Colton had always been into horses. He began riding at age four. He spent most of his free time at the arena. He landed an equestrian scholarship and excelled in college.

Colton was killed one day in a freak accident, caught between two horses spooked by the sudden appearance of a low-flying plane. He had just turned 20.

"At night, all I can think about is Colton. I've had so many nightmares that now I just expect them. Most nights I don't even want to go to bed," Paul shared.

WHEN SLEEP FLEES FROM US

Sleep disturbances are natural and common after the loss of a loved one. Our normal biorhythms have been upset.

Our system frequently interprets loss as a threat, sending us into fight-or-flight mode. It's hard to rest, sleep, or relax when our brains are sending danger signals to our organ systems.

We try to sleep, but sometimes the quiet gets to us. Our minds spin, and most of our thoughts have to do with our child. We naturally dig up all the old questions. Why did this happen? How? What could I have done? How do I live through this?

Minutes turn into hours. If we're lucky, we drift off from time to time. When we do sleep, we often wake up with a start. Another dream about our child. Perhaps it was a nightmare and we wake in a panic. Maybe it was a good dream, and we open our eyes to the terrible disappointment of reality.

Many think dreams are an outlet used by our subconscious to work through what the conscious mind cannot. If so, dreams can be another avenue whereby we process our grief. No wonder we dream of our child. We love and miss them.

Sleep deprivation is said to be the most basic form of torture. Over time, it can begin to take its toll on our bodies and our health.

Most of us need help dealing with the confusion, pain, and anger that so often leads to insomnia and sleep disturbances. None of us should be alone with our nightmares. We're suffering enough already.

Lack of peace, safety, security, and closure usually results in lack of sleep. Sleep disturbances are a natural and common experience for hearts shattered by child loss.

"Even in my sleep, I think of you. I miss you."

QUESTIONS TO CONSIDER AND
AN EXERCISE TO TRY:

Have you experienced changes in your sleep since your child died? How so?

Have you had dreams or nightmares about your child and his / her death? If so, describe one that has made an impression on you.

Sleep disturbances are common. Processing your grief and moving back toward healthy sleep patterns is important. Here are some possible action steps in that direction:

- **Breathe:** Practice breathing deeply, especially right before bed (see the exercise in chapter 6 for details on deep breathing).

- **Talk:** Talk about your dreams with someone you trust. Be as honest and specific as possible. "Getting it out" is important.

- **Write:** Write your nightmares and dreams down. If you're more artistic, draw or paint them. This slows down the mind and emotions and helps us process the experience.

A determined focus to practice these three things — Breathe, Talk, Write — can make a big difference over time. Stay with it. You'll be glad you did.

FROM A FELLOW GRIEVING PARENT:

"Sleep can be tough. Our minds are never quiet. Grab naps when you can. If you can't sleep, rest. Just resting has its benefits."

CHAPTER 22

IDENTIFICATION SYMPTOMS:
"WHAT'S GOING ON?"

---

*"Every time we make the decision to love someone,
we open ourselves to great suffering."*

— Henri Nouwen

"I BEGAN HAVING PALPITATIONS, TIGHTNESS in the chest, and chest pains about two months after Sandy's death," Wanda said. "I've never had heart issues. My diet is good. I exercise and am in good shape. The doctors can't find anything wrong. What's going on?"

Wanda's daughter Sandy was born with a heart murmur. Growing up, she was bothered by episodes of rapid heartbeat that would nearly immobilize her. Doctors treated and monitored her condition into adulthood. One Saturday morning, she collapsed and never regained consciousness. Sandy left behind two small children. She was 36.

"Why is this happening? I live my life shaking in fear, waiting for the next blow," Wanda shared.

EXPERIENCING WHAT OUR CHILD EXPERIENCED

As we discussed previously, many people experience new

or strange bodily sensations or symptoms during their grief process. Grief affects us not only emotionally and mentally, but physically as well. Sometimes as parents, we can so identify with our children that we experience symptoms similar to those of our child when they died.

Wanda had what appeared to be cardiac symptoms soon after her daughter died of a heart condition. Tests revealed that Wanda's symptoms did not have their root in disease or illness. As Wanda intentionally worked through her grief (personal grief work, support groups, and some grief counseling), her symptoms diminished and eventually disappeared.

Yes, it was grief.

We identify with our kids in many ways. They occupy some premier real estate in our hearts. Sometimes we can miss them so badly and want to be with them so much that we begin to feel some of what they might have experienced.

Connection with our kids runs deep. Sometimes it seems downright mystical, and certainly spiritual. Who knows what unseen connections occur at the soul and spirit level?

We feel our child's death in the deepest parts of our being. We internalize and experience it in all kinds of ways — dreams, nightmares, flashbacks, and even similar physical sensations and symptoms as our child experienced.

Experiencing physical distress as part of the grief process is natural and common. Working through our grief in a healthy manner is an important way we can love our child and honor their memory.

"Sometimes I feel so connected to you. I wouldn't want it any other way."

AN EXERCISE TO CONSIDER:

List any new, exacerbated, or strange physical symptoms you've experienced since the death of your child.

How many of these do you believe are related to your child's death and the stress of the grieving process?

Are any of these symptoms similar to something your child might have experienced?

Grieving in a responsible and healthy way is crucial to taking care of yourself during this time. Please remember these three keys: **Breathe, Talk, Write.** If you are diligent about processing your grief in these three ways, you will reap great benefits over time.

FROM A FELLOW GRIEVING PARENT:

"Illnesses and weird symptoms can be scary.
Listen to your body. Rest. Do what you can to take
care of you. Your child would want that."

CHAPTER 23

FATIGUE: "I'M TIRED ALL THE TIME"

> *"I am worn out from my groaning.*
> *All night long I flood my bed with weeping*
> *and drench my couch with tears."*
>
> — *King David of Israel*

"I'M TIRED ALL THE TIME. I can barely put one foot in front of the other. Bruce is the same way. Exhaustion has become a way of life," Carla said.

Carla and Bruce's sons Blake and Barrett were practically inseparable. Two years apart, they grew up as boys will—competing, fighting, cooperating, and having great adventures together. The family lived on a large piece of land out in the country, giving the boys lots of room to roam and explore. They loved their mini-kingdom.

One Saturday, the boys were out riding their ATVs. Inattention led to a loss of control and they collided. Barrett was killed instantly. Blake died a day later in the hospital. They were 13 and 15.

"Life is heavy now. Last night at dinner, I was so exhausted that I could barely chew. Fatigue has taken over our lives," Carla shared.

GRIEF TAKES INCREDIBLE ENERGY

Losing a child is like being hit by a bus. It immobilizes us. The shock waves are immense, and roll over us again and again, relentless and debilitating. Some days, we can barely lift our heads.

Chronic fatigue, even exhaustion, is a common and natural experience for those in heavy grief.

We wake in the morning and it smacks us again. Our child is gone. The shock stuns us. We close our eyes and sigh.

We rise and attempt to do life. We drag from room to room, place to place, task to task. There is little to no heart in what we do. How could there be? Our heart is shattered and in a million pieces.

We put on a mask and fake it through the day. Others are aware of our pain, but don't know what to do with it. Relationships become awkward, tentative, and different.

At work, we go through the motions. Our performance isn't what it was. We're more irritable and erratic. We wonder what others are thinking.

Perhaps we have other children. They are grieving too. We can't handle ourselves right now, so how in the world do we love them through this? Our backs are broken. The thought of shouldering any more weight — even an ounce more — is terrifying.

Numb. Dazed. Fatigued. Exhausted. Our bodies are feeling it. Grief is terribly draining.

"Missing you is exhausting. I'll be patient and take my time."

QUESTIONS TO CONSIDER:

How has your energy level changed since the death of your child? Describe it.

Do you get frustrated with yourself for being tired or exhausted? How so?

SOME SUGGESTIONS:

Grief is incredibly demanding. Fatigue is the natural result. Here are some possible action steps to help manage this:

- Make taking care of yourself a high priority. Focus on nutrition, rest, and exercise. Let these things rise to the top of your list.

- Downgrade your expectations of yourself. If you're a list person, limit each day to three things, and tackle them in the order of importance, not urgency. Most of us in grief have to "do less." Pace yourself.

- Be patient with yourself. This isn't a common cold that will resolve itself in a few days. Recovery often feels slow. Time doesn't heal all wounds, but healing does take time—lots of it.

You will always grieve on some level, but the grief will change. Handle today, this hour, this moment. One moment, one baby step at a time.

FROM A FELLOW GRIEVING PARENT:

"Getting to know your own body is important in this process. If you pay attention, you can learn the signals that say you need a break."

CHAPTER 24

CLUMSINESS: "I BUMP INTO WALLS"

"Without you, I seem to have no stability, anywhere."

— Unknown

"I TRIP. I BUMP INTO walls. I'm an old athlete and pride myself on my physique and coordination. Suddenly I feel like a clumsy oaf," Barbara said.

Barbara's son Thomas was an intelligent, sensitive, and creative kid. He took to art right away and pursued it passionately through college. Thomas was good, perhaps even great. His work began to be noticed.

Thomas was thrilled and excited, but also felt the pressure to perform and produce. That pressure increased over time. Anxiety and depression set in. Late one Sunday evening, Thomas took his own life. He was 29.

"I miss him. I can't even look at his art right now," Barbara sighed. "I'll never understand why. Never. Ever."

GRIEF CAN MAKE US CLUMSY

The loss of a child affects every nook and cranny of our being. Our minds, hearts, bodies, work, and relationships are all impacted. As part of the physical toll, many report clumsiness or lack of coordination.

Like Barbara, we can find ourselves bumping into things and people. We can trip over our own two feet. Something feels a little "off" physically. We're no longer in sync with our bodies.

We stumble. We fall. We burn ourselves while cooking. We have a car accident, or some near misses. We go through red lights and stop signs without even seeing them. We slip in the bathroom. We turn too quickly and twist a knee. We slip off the treadmill or drop a weight on our foot. We break things.

Grief is sucking much of our energy. Our jobs, tasks, and relationships get at best a distracted and fatigued version of ourselves. This trickles down to our coordination, depth perception, and sense of personal space.

We wonder what's happening to us. Is something wrong? Have we contracted a disease? Do we have a tumor? Probably not. When grief affects our bodies, our coordination often takes a hit.

"I'm getting clumsy. I stumble around, missing you."

QUESTIONS TO CONSIDER:

Have you noticed a change in your coordination since your child died? How so?

Does this new clumsiness trouble you? Are there steps you think you can take to help minimize it?

As you move through the grieving process, this new clumsiness should diminish over time. In the meantime, do what you know to do to process things well.

REMEMBER AND PRACTICE
"BREATHE, TALK, WRITE":

- **Breathe:** Keep practicing this, at least once a day. Practice makes permanent, and when deep breathing becomes a habit, you'll be able to use it in almost any situation.

- **Talk:** Talk about what's going on inside. Talk out loud to yourself. Talk to others. Get around people who know grief (support groups, grief counselor, therapists, ministers, etc.) and share.

- **Write:** Journal. Write letters to your child. Get what you're feeling, thinking, and experiencing on paper. Those who make writing a habit usually experience great benefits in the long run. Again, if you're more artistic, draw, paint, or sculpt. Be creative.

Some clumsiness and coordination issues are common and natural for those adjusting to a heavy loss. We've been shattered. The effects are pervasive.

FROM A FELLOW GRIEVING PARENT:

"Now that the worst has happened, we expect everything bad to be permanent. It's not. Much of it will pass."

CHAPTER 25

ANXIETY-DEPRESSION: "I'M PANICKY AND DEPRESSED, TOO!"

"Today my forest is dark. The trees are sad and all the butterflies have broken wings."

— *Raine Cooper*

"I HAVE PANIC ATTACKS. THEY come out of nowhere. Now I walk around anxious, waiting for the next attack to descend. It's like being in a war," Patty said.

"I get anxious, then depressed about being anxious, and then anxious about being depressed," Dave chimed in.

Patty and Dave's daughter Brittany was their only child. She grew into a lovely and poised young woman. She excelled in academics through college and graduate school and landed a fantastic job in a great company. She quickly settled into her new, big-city life.

Brittany began her days by running in the park. One morning she didn't come back. The police found her a few hours later, slain by an unknown assailant. She was 27.

"It's unbelievable, even now. What kind of world do we live in where these things happen?" Patty asked.

ANXIETY AND DEPRESSION MAKE
A CHALLENGING COMBO

Experiencing some anxiety and depression in times of grief is natural and common. We tend to consider them opposites, but they often go together. Though we think of them as primarily emotional issues, this anxiety-depression combo can also be our physiology expressing itself.

Each of us is unique. All of us have a somewhat different, one-of-a-kind biochemistry operating in our brains. Much of this is genetic, but also shaped by our background and life experiences.

In many cases, both anxiety and depression are sprung by a specific trigger — a visual, sound, smell, taste, place, person, or situation. There are other times, however, when our personal biochemistry sets us up for fight-or-flight even when no trigger seems to be present.

Perhaps we have a predisposition to anxiety or depression. Maybe our early life and childhood revealed a high base level of one, the other, or both. It's like our bodies suddenly betray us. Randomly and out of the blue, anxiety or depression descends upon us and almost immediately takes on a life of its own.

Many describe these episodes of panic or depression as coming upon them from the outside, rather than emerging from within them. No matter how they come (trigger or no trigger), or from where (inside or outside), anxiety and depression often come together. Depression and anxiety can be two sides of the same coin.

This is hard to understand and even more challenging to navigate. Learning to recognize, acknowledge, and begin to address this 2-sided coin is important in the grief process.

*"Panic and depression descend from nowhere.
I'll honor you with how I deal with them."*

QUESTIONS TO CONSIDER:

Have you experienced this anxiety-depression combo in your grief? Can you describe what it's like for you?

What has been helpful to you with anxiety-depression so far? What has NOT been helpful?

A POSSIBLE ACTION STEP:

Anxiety-depression can appear seemingly randomly, coming primarily from our personal biochemistry. If this is the case for you, it may be time to consider contacting your doctor or mental health professional. If this 2-sided coin is partially or mostly physiological, medication can be beneficial for some. The ultimate goal is to process and adjust to this terrible loss in the healthiest way possible. If biochemistry is significantly involved, medication can assist us in getting to the point where we can process this loss and deal better with the resulting grief.

Taking care of yourself emotionally, mentally, and physically is a wonderful and powerful way to love and honor your child.

FROM A FELLOW GRIEVING PARENT:

*"Try to accept where you are at. Feel the
grief instead of fighting against it."*

WHERE WE'VE BEEN AND WHERE WE'RE GOING...

Grief hits our bodies too.

In this section, we've discussed the pervasive physical impact we can experience in the grief process. Our bodies are feeling the power of our loss. Headaches, stomach issues, heart concerns, pain, dizziness, clumsiness, more frequent colds, and minor illnesses are common complaints. Diet changes, sleep disturbances, and nightmares are not unusual.

We've looked at some physical challenges we might face and talked about how to deal with them. Making self-care a priority is key to grieving in a healthy and responsible manner. We need to not only take our hearts and minds seriously, but our bodies as well.

What are our bodies telling us? What changes do we need to make to live healthy lives in the midst of this demanding season?

In addition to our hearts, minds, and bodies, the death of a child can have powerful and lasting spiritual impact. We'll discuss this in the next section.

PART FOUR:

THE SPIRITUAL IMPACT

THE DEATH OF A CHILD is powerful. It hits our whole being, affecting us emotionally, mentally, physically, and spiritually. In this section, we'll look at the spiritual impact this heavy loss can have on grieving parents.

Spiritual confusion is common. Many experience anger with God. Some have intense wondering and questions about death and the afterlife. Others get mired in deep guilt, unable to forgive themselves. Still others grow bitter, unable or unwilling to forgive self, others, or God for what happened.

Many grow spiritually numb. God seems distant. Our faith feels limp and lifeless. Some experience deep doubt about the truth of long-held beliefs and convictions.

This spiritual upheaval can be disturbing and shocking. How do we navigate this?

The roller-coaster continues. Keep yourself strapped in. Hold on tight. Keep an open mind and heart. Read on...

CHAPTER 26

SPIRITUAL CONFUSION: "I'M NOT SURE WHAT I BELIEVE ANYMORE"

"The greatest pain comes from leaving."

— Henri Nouwen

"I USED TO BE SURE about a lot of things. Not now. I'm confused. I'm not sure what I believe anymore," Tony shared.

Tony's son Drake was the oldest of four boys. He was the leader and mastermind of the sibling crew, forming vast armies and leading them in heroic battles. With Drake as their general, they conquered every enemy they faced.

Then came leukemia.

Drake took it like a champ. He faced his treatment like the little soldier he trained himself to be. He fought valiantly. Drake died at home, with his mom holding one hand and his dad the other. He was 12.

"How could this happen? Why? Where is God in this?" Tony asked.

SPIRITUAL CONFUSION IS COMMON

The spiritual impact of a child's death is massive. For many parents, it raises deeply buried, long-held questions (along with some new ones) about God, the spiritual world, heaven, and the afterlife.

Our hearts have been shattered. Spiritually, we can be deeply shaken. Many of our beliefs may be challenged. Our spiritual wonderings can be intensified.

One thing is certain—our spiritual life, whatever we define that to be, will change. It cannot stay the same. We will either choose to grow deeper into our beliefs, distance ourselves from them, or adopt some new ones (or a combo of all these).

Our hearts and minds desperately need to make spiritual sense of this loss. We do this through whatever faith-lens we're looking through. If our belief system doesn't supply adequate, emotionally satisfying answers, comfort, and hope, we'll naturally begin to question things.

Some are vocal about their spiritual questioning. Others are intensely private. Whichever the case, most of us intuitively know that no answer will completely satisfy our broken, shattered, and bleeding hearts. We miss our child. We want them back. To expect ourselves to see things with decently clear perspective is unrealistic (or perhaps impossible).

Our normal view of the world can be rattled, torn, or completely dismantled by this traumatic loss. Spiritual confusion and questioning during this time are natural and common.

"I wonder about a lot now. I'm sure of some things, but less sure of others."

QUESTIONS TO CONSIDER:

Have you found yourself wondering about or questioning your spiritual beliefs since the death of your child? How so?

What are your largest spiritual questions at the moment?

AN EXERCISE TO TRY:

Some have clearly defined spiritual beliefs. Others do not. The important thing is processing how this loss is impacting us spiritually. To help with this, let's go back to the **BIG 3: Breathe, Talk, Write.**

- **Breathe.** Keep practicing deep breathing at least once a day. When you find yourself feeling overwhelmed, find a chair, get quiet, and initiate deep breathing.

- **Talk.** It's important to verbalize what's going on in us spiritually. Talk with a trusted friend, grief counselor, therapist, or minister. Sharing what you're thinking and feeling may be more important than finding answers. Process those doubts and questions verbally.

- **Write.** Journal about what's going on spiritually. Write a letter to God. If you're not into writing, draw, paint, or sculpt what's happening inside. Creative expression helps greatly in processing the spiritual impact of your child's death.

You will not be the same. You know this. As you genuinely seek answers, truth has a way of surfacing over time.

FROM A FELLOW GRIEVING PARENT:

*"Hang on. Survive. I wandered, but in
the end my faith saved me."*

CHAPTER 27

ANGER WITH GOD: "HOW COULD GOD LET THIS HAPPEN?"

"Something inside this heart has died."

— *Unknown*

"I'M ANGRY WITH GOD. HOW could he let this happen?" Corey asked.

Corey's daughter Kailey was a spunky, honest, and serious kid. In school, she earned the title of "Bully Hunter" for her aggressive protection of outcasts and underdogs. Kailey's convictions made her incredibly popular, earning her Homecoming Queen honors.

One night on the way home from a dance, a drunk driver jumped the median and ran head on into Kailey and her date. Both teens were killed. Kailey was 17.

"I'm angry at the driver, the dance organizers, the school, God, and the universe," Corey shared. "This is all wrong. This should never, ever happen. Never."

ANGER WITH GOD IS COMMON IN GRIEF

Anger with God about our child's death is a common

reaction for our shattered hearts. The questions begin to tumble from our wounded, angry souls.

How can God allow this? Couldn't he have prevented it? Why didn't he?

How does God feel about this? Does he care? How much?

Did we do something to cause this? Is this payback or punishment for something we did or didn't do? Is this karma? Is it fate? Is it a random, senseless event? Is it some kind of sick joke?

The questions go on and on. We want to make sense of our loss, and part of that is trying to determine who's ultimately responsible for what happened. Many of us come to the conclusion that the buck stops with God.

Anger with God is taboo for some. We might fear spiritual reprisal (either from God or other people). But if God is God, he knows we're angry. If he is concerned about us, then surely he would value us honestly expressing our hearts to him.

Relationships where we don't share don't deepen and grow. When we hide, relationships become distant, and at best end up being a masquerade. This would be true of a relationship with God as well.

Anger with God is common among parents who have lost a child. As we deal with that anger and express it responsibly, we give our hearts a chance to adjust and heal.

"I'm angry with God. I'll honor you, my child,
by dealing responsibly with that anger."

QUESTIONS TO CONSIDER:

Have you experienced anger with God during your grief process? If so, describe what that was like.

Have you expressed your anger to God? If not, what's holding you back? If so, describe what that was like.

AN EXERCISE TO CONSIDER USING BREATHE, TALK, WRITE:

- **Breathe:** When you find yourself angry, begin deep breathing. Focus on your breathing as much as possible.

- **Talk:** Consider talking about your anger with God (or spiritual anger at something else), with a friend you trust, a mentor, a minister, a grief counselor or therapist. Express yourself honestly and be as specific as possible.

- **Write:** Write a letter to God about your anger. Don't hold back. Let it out. Write numerous letters if necessary. Getting the anger down on paper helps process this powerful emotion.

FROM A FELLOW GRIEVING PARENT:

"It's okay to be mad at God. I was, and still am sometimes. As long as I'm honest about it, my heart can handle it."

CHAPTER 28

SPIRITUAL SEARCHING:
"Where is She Now?"

"Not all those who wander are lost."

— J.R.R. Tolkien

"I wish I could see her somehow. I want to know where she is, what it's like, and what she's doing," Connie said.

Connie's daughter Libby was a wild child. She experimented with drugs early and became an addict. After hitting bottom, she checked herself into a rehab center and got clean. She went to college and pursued a degree in social work, fueled by a passion to help others.

One night Libby received a distress call from a friend. When she arrived on the scene, she got caught in the crossfire of a drug deal gone wrong. Libby was 19.

"She was the bravest person I've known. I'm honored to be her mother. I hope I'll see her again," Connie said.

LOSS OFTEN LEADS TO SPIRITUAL SEARCHING

Previously we discussed how the death of a child can create all kinds of spiritual questioning. Those questions can launch us on a search for answers.

Did our child just cease to exist? Are they alive in another dimension? Are they a spirit now, or do they have a body too? Would we recognize them?

Where are they now? What are they doing? Who are they with? Are they happy? How does all this work? Can we know anything for sure?

Some are sure about what's ahead. Others don't claim certainty, but choose to believe the best they can imagine based on what seems right to them. Others have fairly undeveloped belief systems and have to wade through a lot of uncertainty.

No matter who we are, we all believe something. And we all have some ideas about what happens after death.

We are also relational beings. When someone we love dies, our hearts crack. Separation from those we love is excruciatingly hard. We need comfort and hope. So it's not surprising that most of us choose beliefs that provide these two necessities. If there is no comfort, we are alone and completely crushed. If there is no hope, we are bereft indeed.

The death of a child can confirm long-held beliefs or smash them into a thousand pieces. Our loss can launch us on a search for spiritual truth or drive us into skepticism. Our spiritual beliefs, in order for us to hold them, must weather and ultimately pass the test of deep personal loss and suffering.

Spiritual searching is common in times of heavy loss and personal pain. For many of us, it's the natural result of having a broken heart.

"I want to know about you, my child. I need answers. I will search for them."

QUESTIONS TO CONSIDER:

Have you found yourself searching for spiritual answers since the death of your child? If so, what answers are you seeking?

Are there spiritual beliefs that you are certain of at this point? If so, what are they?

POSSIBLE ACTION STEPS:

Take a moment and list the spiritual questions you want answers to.

Once you complete this list, consider using **Breathe, Talk, Write** to process your questions further.

- **Breathe:** Practice breathing deeply while reading over your list. Take your time. Try to relax.

- **Talk:** Share your list of spiritual questions with someone you trust. Voicing these and being real with others is a huge part of healthy grieving.

- **Write:** Spend time writing your spiritual questions and the answers you're seeking. You could write letters to God about this. Honestly express where you are. Writing makes things more concrete. If drawing, painting, or sculpting helps more, do that. Our hearts need to express themselves.

FROM A FELLOW GRIEVING PARENT:

"Figure out what you believe and why. What you believe must be bigger than your loss."

CHAPTER 29

SPIRITUAL NUMBNESS:
"I FEEL DEAD INSIDE"

"There is an empty place within me where my heart was once."

— George Martin

"EVERYTHING GOOD SEEMS FAR AWAY. I'm emotionally and spiritually paralyzed. I feel dead inside," Jack shared.

Jack's daughter Chloe was a daddy's girl. She clung to Jack wherever he went. He adored her.

Chloe grew up in a stable and loving home. She confronted the usual, daunting challenges teens face and emerged from them fairly unscathed. She married her high school sweetheart. They had three kids, two boys and a girl.

One day Chloe was returning from grocery shopping. A thunderstorm had been raging for hours. Chloe's car hydroplaned, and she lost control. She was killed in a multi-car pile-up. She was 34.

"Dads protect their daughters, but I couldn't protect her," Jack said, gazing into my eyes.

DEEP LOSS CAN PRODUCE SPIRITUAL NUMBNESS

After the death of a child, many report a sort of spiritual

numbness or fatigue. Trying to make sense of what appears to be senseless can be spiritually exhausting.

All of us have a faith of some kind, even if it's not clearly defined. We all believe something about ourselves, life, the world, God, the spiritual realm, and the afterlife. In tough times, most of us either lean heavily on our faith, begin to question it, or both.

The death of a child raises deep questions. We search for answers. Our emotions are varied, complicated, and frustrating. It's easy to become spiritually frustrated too. We experience overwhelm, and spiritual fatigue sets in.

We engage in our usual spiritual activities, whatever they might be, or perhaps we distance ourselves from them. As with the rest of life, we might find ourselves going through the spiritual motions, but feeling little to nothing. What was once powerfully meaningful can now seem dull, drab, and empty.

We can become spiritually numb. This isn't necessarily negative, but rather the natural result of having our hearts shattered and experiencing grief overload over a period of time.

Spiritual numbness can protect us. It can provide a much needed break from the intense emotional assault and the incessant search for answers. This numbness can be a valuable spiritual rest stop along the grief highway. For most, it's a temporary state. We pause there for a while, and then re-engage when we're ready. We all need rest— not just physical, but spiritual as well.

For some, spiritual numbness can be unnerving and frightening. In most cases, however, this is a natural part of the grief process about which we can say, "This too shall pass."

*"Losing you is spiritually exhausting. I'll honor
you by taking my heart seriously."*

QUESTIONS TO CONSIDER:

Have you experienced spiritual numbness since the death
of your child? If so, what was it like?

How did you respond to being spiritually numb? What
seemed to help, and what didn't?

AN EXERCISE TO TRY:

Write a letter or poem (you choose to whom, knowing this
is a letter you will never send) describing how you sense
you are doing spiritually. Are you experiencing spiritual
fatigue or numbness? What is that like?

After writing, consider talking with someone about what
you wrote—a trusted friend, mentor, minister, counselor,
etc. Sharing our grief is important, both for us and others.

Spiritual fatigue and numbness are common for those who
have lost of child. Most often this is temporary. This too
shall pass.

FROM A FELLOW GRIEVING PARENT:

*"This will probably be the worst thing you will ever
go through. Hold on to your faith and your memories.
Nothing can take those away from you."*

CHAPTER 30

GUILT-PUNISHMENT:"GOD WON'T FORGIVE ME, AND I CAN'T FORGIVE MYSELF"

*"But of all Heaven's lessons, guilt isn't one of
them. You don't need to hold on to it.
It doesn't need to be a practice and it shouldn't be your life."*

— *Tessa Shaffer*

"I KNOW IT'S MY FAULT. Now I'm being punished. I can't make this right. What can I do?" Melissa choked through her tears.

Melissa's son Carter was her third child. He came out screaming, and (according to Melissa) never stopped talking. He grew like a weed.

One hot summer day, the family was in the back yard enjoying their pool. Melissa turned away for a moment. When she looked back, Carter was gone. She frantically searched before finally noticing him on the bottom of the pool. Carter was three years old.

"I should have been watching. God will never forgive me for this. And I'll never, ever forgive myself. Because of me, Carter is dead," she said with a cold stare.

WHEN WE FEEL GUILTY, WE PUNISH OURSELVES

As parents, we're responsible for loving, nurturing, providing for, and protecting our children — to the best of our limited ability. When our child dies, especially if they are young, we feel responsible. How could this happen on our watch? We missed something. We should have been there. We should have known.

We add guilt and remorse to the already unbearable pain of losing a child. We begin to punish ourselves, consciously or subconsciously. The shame cripples us. Even if our faith is deep and solid, some of us have trouble raising our eyes to heaven, or even whispering a prayer.

Someone is to blame. Someone should pay. We're the parents. Who's more responsible than we are?

Perhaps we see this tragedy as punishment for the things we did or didn't do. Maybe we believe our child was taken from us because we weren't good enough. We've messed up too much and crossed a line somewhere, and now God, karma, fate, or the universe has given us what we deserve.

Underneath it all is the shaky belief that if we had been better parents, better people, this would not have happened. We're bad and our child is dead. Forgiveness is impossible.

In grief and in life, we often confuse being responsible with being in control. That never works, because it's simply not true. We influence much, but are never "in control" when it comes to relationships, other people, or circumstances. We don't even cause our own hearts to beat.

We aren't perfect. Far from it. We aren't omniscient (all-knowing) — not even close. We're not omnipresent (everywhere at once), but limited to being in one small spot on this planet at any given time. We're not omnipotent (all-powerful) — not by a long shot. Yet, as parents, we sometimes expect ourselves to be all of these.

Whatever our belief system, it must provide somehow for the resolution of guilt. Forgiveness must be included and available, or else we are lost and without hope.

Blaming ourselves is a common parental reaction to the death of a child. But it is not healthy, and hinders our recovery and healing.

"Part of loving and honoring you is forgiving myself. I'm working on that."

AN EXERCISE TO CONSIDER:

This exercise will take a little time. It may be emotional. That's okay. We're processing some tough stuff here.

Take a moment and list anything you feel responsible for related to the death of your child. Be as specific as possible.

Do you believe you can be forgiven? What would it look like to forgive yourself?

Write a letter or poem to your child expressing the guilt you feel. Be as specific as you can. Consider asking forgiveness from God, your child, and perhaps your family.

Now, imagine your child in front of you, and read this letter out loud.

When done, go back to the letter and write at the bottom, "I forgive myself." Read it out loud.

We often need to forgive ourselves over and over again, each time at a deeper level. Keep forgiving. Keep releasing yourself. This is part of healthy grieving that honors your child and those you love.

FROM A FELLOW GRIEVING PARENT:

"I have two sons. One lives in heaven, and the other is here. I have peace now, but I had to forgive myself first. This may take time, but you must do this too."

WHERE WE'VE BEEN AND WHERE WE'RE GOING...

The death of a child has profound spiritual impact. This loss in itself is a deeply spiritual experience. We can respond to it in a number of ways.

We've discussed some of the spiritual ramifications grieving parents deal with. None of us are the same, and our faith — whatever it was — will not be the same either. We've been deeply affected spiritually by our child, and by their death. This is natural. How we deal with the spiritual stress is important.

Next, we'll look at how this loss impacts our relationships. Since our world has been abruptly altered, our relationships will change too.

PART FIVE:

THE RELATIONAL IMPACT

THE LOSS OF A CHILD affects everything. Our emotions, minds, bodies, and souls are stunned and shaken.

The world is not the same.

Our lives are not the same.

We are not the same.

Our relationships will not be the same either.

In this section, we'll look at the relational impact of our loss. Some people will pledge great support, but distance themselves over time. Others will be well-meaning, but say and do unhelpful things. Still others will come closer and play a larger role than ever.

Some people will be toxic. Others will be safe and healing. New people will surface, and become key influences in our lives.

Yes, everything has changed. How do we handle this? Breathe deeply. Read on...

CHAPTER 31

UNSUPPORTIVE FAMILY: "FAMILY HARDLY TALKS TO US NOW"

"This hurts because you mattered."

— Unknown

"FAMILY HAS BEEN DISAPPOINTING," AARON said. "We heard all the usual stuff. 'We're with you. We'll be there for you. Anything you need,' and all that. Now they hardly talk to us, except to say that we should be over this by now."

Aaron and his wife Stacey longed for children. They tried for years with no luck. They began fertility treatments. After two early miscarriages, they finally maintained a pregnancy into the eighth month.

Then a routine doctor visit revealed that their son Donnie's heart was no longer beating.

"We were devastated. The pain was and is unbelievable. On top of that, we not only feel alone, but rejected," Aaron shared.

FAMILY CAN DISAPPOINT US

When loss hits, things change. The death of a child shatters our world and jostles all our relationships, especially those with family. This is natural and common in grief.

We expect support, love, and acceptance from family. The reality may be different. Instead of being with us in our loss, they may try to fix us, help us feel better, or somehow rescue us from our pain.

In addition, we may have unspoken expectations of family — what level and kind of support they will give, how much they should contact, and how they will behave. If these expectations are high, chances are we'll be disappointed.

Caring family members don't like to see us in pain. Sometimes our pain can trigger theirs. They can find themselves increasingly uncomfortable. They don't know what to do or say. Perhaps they end up hurting us. Maybe they disappear. To us it feels like they're trying to either wound us further or abandon us to our pain.

Over time, this disconnect with family can grow. The distance between us can widen. Relationships can become estranged or even severed. We experience even more loss.

We're not the same, and we won't ever be the same again. Some family members don't understand that. They don't like it. It messes with their world.

We've been changed forever by our child and their death. Our relationships will change too, one way or the other.

These relational changes can be tumultuous, frustrating, and exhausting.

"Some family members don't understand.
I will never stop loving you."

QUESTIONS TO CONSIDER:

Have you noticed some family distancing themselves from you or trying to fix you? How has this affected you?

If your unsupportive family member was in front of you right now, what would you like to be able to say?

AN EXERCISE TO TRY:

Consider writing a letter (that you will never send!) to an unsupportive family member. Tell them how you feel. Be as honest and as uncensored as possible. Get it out.

Relational upset among family members is not uncommon in grief. Do what you can to grieve responsibly and in a healthy manner.

FROM A FELLOW GRIEVING PARENT:

"Take your time and grieve your way. Don't apologize for your loss or your grief. Above all, talk about your child and encourage others to do the same."

CHAPTER 32

SUPPORTIVE FAMILY: "FAMILY HAS MADE ALL THE DIFFERENCE"

"Grief turns out to be a place none of us know until we reach it."

— Joan Didion

"I DON'T KNOW WHAT I would have done without my family. They have been super-supportive," Andrea said.

Andrea's son Dade was born premature and struggled greatly for most of his life. His health issues were almost non-stop. Andrea joked that their family van ought to be able to drive from their home to the doctor's office and hospital all by itself.

Yet, Dade seemed to be a happy kid. Even when he felt lousy, he still managed a smile.

Over time, Dade's body began to show signs of wearing out. They showered Dade with love as he slowly slipped away. He was five years old.

"I was a basket case. I could hardly think, and barely talk. Family members kept on top of things — calling, texting, checking on me, and doing what they could to prop me up. Their love slowly injected life back into my soul," Andrea shared.

FAMILY SUPPORT CAN MAKE A HUGE DIFFERENCE

In most grievers' experience, some family members are supportive, while others are less than helpful. Some show up, know how to hold their tongues, and seem to be more comfortable with grief. Others run away, try to fix, or attempt to pull us out of our pain.

Most of us have at least one family member who has the prized ability to come into a crisis and love people who are hurting. These folks may not say much, but they're available, and their presence is comforting.

Some family cry with us. They enter in and get their hands dirty. They babysit, make meals, and run errands. They're willing to handle routine business so that we don't have to. They don't force themselves on us, but are willing and ready.

They call. They text. They listen. These relatives are incredibly helpful and encouraging. They bolster our sense of hope. They don't push. They don't pull. They merely walk alongside us.

Some have tons of supportive family. Others have a few. Still others have none.

All of us have a different set of needs and circumstances. What's supportive and when isn't a one-size-fits-all proposition. This is difficult (even impossible) for some family members to navigate.

Do we have any specific expectations? Do we want family to text, call, or come over? Who? How often? What kind of help do we want and need? From whom? How much?

Of course, we're in a grief state where discussing these things seems about as doable as a solo climb of Mount Everest. However, if we can possibly carve out time and energy to think and communicate about these things, we will usually reap good results.

Supportive family make a massive impact in our grief process. If we don't have this, thank goodness there are other loving, compassionate, and caring people out there.

"I'm hurting, but don't know what I need.
All I can think about is you."

QUESTIONS TO CONSIDER:

On a scale of 1-to-10 (with 10 being amazing), how supportive has your family been in your grief process?

With regard to family support, what has been helpful to you and what hasn't?

Are there ways family could be more helpful to you now? How so? Be as specific as possible.

Are there family members you are willing to communicate your needs and desires to? Who? How? Can you make a plan to do this?

Some relatives are stellar when disaster strikes. Others aren't. Lean on those who show up and make themselves available. None of us should have to walk this road alone.

FROM A FELLOW GRIEVING PARENT:

"We need people who will sit with us and listen. We need to talk about our child, and are thrilled when others do too."

CHAPTER 33

FRIENDS: "Where Did Everyone Go?"

---

*"If you have ever lost someone very important to
you, then you already know how it feels,
and if you haven't, you cannot possibly imagine it."*

— *Lemony Snicket*

"Where did everyone go? Do we have some kind of
disease? Are we contagious?" Sandra said, fire in her eyes.

Sandra's daughter Sam was their firstborn. Sam and her
little brother Stephen were quite a pair. They were together
a lot and grew up close, the best of friends.

One Saturday they were heading across the street to the
park in their neighborhood. A truck zoomed around the
corner. As if by instinct, Sam yelled and shoved Stephen
out of harm's way. Sam died hours later in the hospital.
She was eight years old.

"At first, we were inundated with support — calls, texts,
and food. People were dropping by at all hours. Then, poof!
Nothing," Sandra continued.

"When we do see friends, it's awkward. They glance at
their phones or their watches. They never bring Sam up or
say her name," Sandra said, as she began to cry.

LOSS CHANGES FRIENDSHIPS

When death strikes, it upends us. It upsets the equilibrium of our lives, including our relationships. Friendships are usually greatly affected.

When a child dies, our friendships are suddenly catapulted into unchartered territory. It's as if we've been transported to some foreign country or alternate dimension. This is our life now, but our friends know nothing about this new, foreboding place.

Perhaps they visit us in this new land of child loss and grief. This scares, even terrifies them. They look at their own kids and shudder. This could happen to them too.

Our old life is gone. For the most part, our friends' lives go on as before. The gap between us widens.

Some people we counted on disappear. Maybe they're avoiding us. Perhaps they're just going on with their own busy and demanding lives. The result is the same. They're not there.

Others who were on the periphery move closer, wondering what they can do to help. Their eyes reveal compassionate hearts.

Strangers appear. Some know grief and are well-acquainted with loss. Perhaps they've even lost children. New friendships bud. Over time, they take root and grow.

Loss alters friendships. Some may evaporate, but others will thrive and deepen. Our hearts are shattered, but we can still feel supported, cared for, and loved.

We are not alone.

"Some friends have disappeared. The ones I need will step up. I am not alone."

QUESTIONS TO CONSIDER:

How have your friendships been affected by the death of your child and your grief process?

What do you sense you need most from your friends right now? Do they know this? Is there a way you can share this with them?

AN EXERCISE TO TRY:

Write a letter to your friends (in general) about how they have reacted to you since the death of your child (another letter you will not send!). Be honest and uncensored. End the letter by describing what you hope for and need from your friends now, from here on out.

FROM A FELLOW GRIEVING PARENT:

"A person who has lost a child will never be the same. It would be nice if our friends understood that. But if we don't even understand it, how can they?"

CHAPTER 34

WORK: "Work is Weird"

---

*"You do what you're supposed to do, but
in fact you're not there at all."*

— *Frederick Barthelme*

"I go to work, but I'm not all there. I'm tired. My brain is foggy. I'm on auto-pilot most of the time," Tim shared. "Work is weird. Everything is weird."

Tim's son Ethan was a quiet, introspective kid. He preferred reading and video games to people. He was brilliant, but made average grades in school. He excelled in college, and landed a nice IT job. He was well-liked, but a loner.

At work, he always took the stairs, trying to get all the exercise he could. One Tuesday, he left for lunch and headed to the exit sign. Unknown to Ethan, there was a large spill at the top of the stairs on his floor. He slipped and fell.

His co-workers found him several hours later. Ethan was 28.

"I can't hardly sit at a computer without tearing up. The fact that I work in IT doesn't help," Tim said with a sigh.

LOSS IMPACTS WORK TOO

The loss of a child impacts every area of life. Many of us spend 40 plus hours a week at work. Our jobs will be anything but business as usual.

Grief is exhausting. We're tired. Most of us wake fatigued and trudge through the day as best we can. We tackle complex vocational tasks. We desperately try to keep up with the expectations placed upon us and our own to-do list.

We face people, co-workers, every day. Some smile and pat us on the back. Some ask us how we're doing and try to be sensitive and supportive. Some avoid eye contact, not knowing what to say and terrified they might make things worse somehow. Some try to cheer us up. Everyone senses the huge change. The whole thing is, well, awkward.

Then there are our bosses and supervisors. Some are compassionate, and their primary concern is for us and our well-being. They listen, and treat us like human beings. Others are more concerned about the job, the effect on the bottom line, and our work performance. Some are so wrapped up in their own lives they act as if nothing has happened.

Co-workers are mostly caring and supportive, but their lives haven't changed. They haven't (most likely) experienced the loss of a child. They naturally anticipate that we will rebound from this and be the same people we were before. They have no frame of reference for what we are enduring.

We begin to feel the squeeze of job requirements and expectations. Our own desire to work hard and perform well adds to the burden. Work is tough when we're grieving.

How do we do this? Is it possible to be somewhat

honest and still perform our functions adequately? Should we shut our emotions down at work and compartmentalize our loss somehow? Is there a balance here? What's healthy?

We're all different. All our losses are unique. Our talents, abilities, and jobs are all diverse. We have different co-workers, supervisors, and bosses. In other words, there is no cut-and-dried, works-every-time, one-size-fits-all approach.

There are however, a few things we can consider that might help.

Is it possible to do a sort of pre-emptive strike and inform co-workers how we're doing and what they can expect from us? Here's a possible example:

"As you know, my son Ethan died last week. We're devastated. I know you probably wonder what you can say or do to be supportive. Just be aware that I'm hurting, no matter how I might appear. Please don't ask me how I'm doing during work, or I'll never make it through the day. Smile, pat me on the back, or give me a hug. Feel free to call or text me later. I would love to talk about Ethan and share how I'm doing, but would prefer to do that after work hours. I take my job seriously. I will give all I can to do the best job I can. I'm thankful to be part of this team."

Life is different now, and work is no exception. Finding a way to grieve, be honest, and still meet job expectations is challenging. Experiencing work stress during a time of loss and grief is natural and common. Doing what we can to take care of ourselves and grieve responsibly outside of work will be crucial.

"Work is weird and awkward now. I'll find a way to grieve honestly and still work well."

AN EXERCISE TO TRY:

Think about your job and workplace. What do you want and need to communicate to your boss, supervisor, and co-workers? Make a brief list.

How can your boss, supervisor, and co-workers best support you, both during and outside of work? What do you need from them to help this go well for everyone?

Spend some time and come up with a "statement" like the example in this chapter. Take your time. Be brief, but clear. After you finish, consider showing it to your boss and get his or her input.

When we go to work, the elephant is already in the room. It's best to face it head on and decide how we would like co-workers to interact with us about the death of our child.

FROM A FELLOW GRIEVING PARENT:

"Words are cheap. But a hug can go a long, long way."

CHAPTER 35

PEOPLE OF FAITH: "SOME ARE HELPFUL, SOME AREN'T"

"There is a sacredness in tears. They are not the mark of weakness, but of power. They speak more eloquently than ten thousand tongues."

— *Washington Irving*

"OUR CHURCH HAS BEEN SUPPORTIVE, but it still amazes me what people will say. 'At least he's not suffering...God needed another angel...You still have other children.'" Janice shared. "My son is dead. Platitudes are useless, and hurtful."

Janice's son Kolton was the youngest of four. He was a fast and agile kid. He excelled at almost every sport, but football was his game. He became a star running back in high school and was heavily recruited by universities.

One Friday night his senior year, Kolton was racing down the field, the goal line in sight. He went airborne and attempted to hurdle the only remaining defender. Kolton's feet caught his opponent's helmet, slamming him to the ground head first. He immediately went limp. Attempts to revive him were unsuccessful. He was 17.

"The out-pouring of love has been phenomenal. Many

have been comforting and encouraging. It's these platitude-droppers that get to me. Are they that uncomfortable with pain and death?" Janice asked.

PEOPLE OF FAITH ARE STILL PEOPLE

The loss of a child shakes our relationships, and that includes our interactions with people of faith. Some of these will step up and be supportive way beyond our expectations. Others will disappoint us. Like us, they are imperfect, inconsistent human beings—fallible, scared, and often insecure.

Some people believe they must respond in a specific way to certain situations, almost like a human parrot. They spout out what they think is the prescribed answer. Because they believe their words to be true, they also naively assume they will be comforting and encouraging.

When people make statements without first attempting to hear our pain, we feel violated, unheard, and invisible. Our shattered hearts wriggle and scream with the hurt, and the anger.

Platitudes are empty. We throw words at suffering, as if that will somehow explain it away or push it into hiding. Compassion, on the other hand, is born when we close our mouths and open our hearts.

Some people will be open-mouthed, while others will be open-hearted. No one is perfect. We all suffer from our own brokenness, pain, and vulnerabilities. The key is finding people who tend to be open-hearted most of the time.

Here is a basic guideline for healthy grieving: Get around people who are helpful to you, and limit your exposure to those who aren't. We need people whose hearts are open, perhaps through being shattered like ours.

We need people willing to show up, listen, and serve. We can't afford to entrust our hearts to platitude-lovers, fixers, and cardboard people uncomfortable with pain. Instead, we search for love-driven people in whose presence our wounded souls can rest.

Death is uncomfortable for most people, especially the death of a child. Many stand ready to assist, love, and comfort. A few of these people can make a massive difference in our grief process.

"I need love and understanding. I will look for open hearts to be with me in my grief."

QUESTIONS TO CONSIDER:

What kind of responses have you gotten so far from people of faith (both words and actions)?

How has the death of your child impacted what you believe (about life, yourself, God, the universe, etc)?

What words / actions of others have been most comforting and encouraging to you thus far?

FROM A FELLOW GRIEVING PARENT:

"Don't give others control over your heart. If possible, respond in love. Who needs more regrets?"

CHAPTER 36

MARRIAGE: "WE'RE DRIFTING APART"

"The death of a child not only changes a parent forever, it also permanently alters a couple's marriage...As a couple you must deal with how each of you has changed."

— Cindy Wright

"WE'RE HURTING," MINDY SAID, REFERRING to herself and her husband, Daniel. "I cry. He works in the garage. I go shopping. He drinks beer and watches sports."

Mindy and Daniel's son Andrew was born adventurous. His dad joked that Andy tasted adrenaline at an early age and had been addicted ever since. When he turned 15, Andrew got a motorcycle. He screamed for joy as he screeched away on his first solo ride.

Several hours later, the police were sitting in Mindy and Daniel's living room, delivering the news that every parent dreads. Andrew was dead.

"Losing Andy was bad enough. Now I feel like I'm losing Daniel too. I'm afraid we're drifting apart," Mindy said.

LOSS AFFECTS MARRIAGES

When a child dies, the family changes. All family relationships are affected, including marriages.

Men and women tend to grieve differently. Many men are activity-project grievers. They solve problems, build things, tear stuff apart, exercise heavily, or head to the shooting range. Most women tend to be verbal-relational grievers. They seek connections, have coffee, talk, share, cry, text, and email.

Men do things. Women relate. We speak different grief languages. This makes it even more challenging to communicate well during this time. Finding ways to grieve together is yet another obstacle (or opportunity) we get to face and tackle.

Both spouses are chest-deep in heavy grief. Routines have changed. Emotions are running high. Our usual patterns of touch, physical affection, and sexual intimacy might be disrupted. It can seem like someone threw a grenade into our family and our marriage.

The loss of a child can put great stress on a marriage. Thankfully, there are a few simple things we can do to make a positive difference.

First, we can reaffirm our love and commitment. The words "I love you" are especially powerful now. We need to say them, and then back them up any way we can.

Second, we need to accept that our partner grieves differently than we do. Appreciating our differences is important. We lost the same child, but we do not grieve in the same way.

Third, we need to be aware of danger signs: outside emotional attachments, addictions, affairs, abuse, etc. These unhealthy coping mechanisms are dangerous to any committed relationship. If we notice these things occurring, it's wise to seek outside help. Handling these marital landmines ourselves while immersed in grief is virtually impossible.

Marriages are forever impacted when a child dies. Our goal is to adjust together, while grieving differently. Respect, acceptance, and love must reign if we are to weather this storm intact.

"Grief is hitting my marriage. I will affirm my love, respect our differences, and seek help when needed."

QUESTIONS TO CONSIDER:

Take some time and describe how the death of your child has affected your marriage.

How can you affirm your love and commitment to your partner today? Make a simple plan. Do it.

Work on accepting your partner's style of grieving. How can you show respect for your partner's grief today?

Have you noticed any marital danger signs emerging (addictions, emotional attachments, affairs, abuse, etc.)? If so, who can you reach out to for input (counselor, minister, mentor, etc.)?

FROM A FELLOW GRIEVING PARENT:

"Cling to each other. You can't choose for your partner, but do what you can to draw close during this time."

CHAPTER 37

OUR OTHER KIDS: "How Do We Help Them and Ourselves Too?"

"If you're going through hell, keep going."

-*Winston Churchill*

"Our boys keep us sane and going. If it wasn't for them and my job, I would go crazy," Russell said.

Russell's and Patricia's daughter Talley was their middle child, sandwiched between two sons. She was the princess of their household.

The leukemia was discovered early. The boys had a hard time with their sister being sick all the time. They hated watching her suffer. Talley was a champ, but over time her smile became forced and her spark seemed to be fading.

A residual infection landed Talley in the hospital. The decline was swift, and she died the next morning. She was seven years old.

"It hit the boys hard," Russell continued. "They fought. They acted out. We wanted to help, but had no idea what to do. We all missed her so much."

HELPING OUR KIDS WHILE GRIEVING OURSELVES

When a child dies, their siblings are uniquely affected. One of their own has disappeared, and their absence is palpable and confusing. Their little minds wonder and spin.

What does death mean? Does it hurt? Did only a part of her die? Where is she now? Will she come back? Will we see her again? Will she grow up too, or will she always be this age? What's it like to die? Will I die? Will it be soon? Will I get sick too?

The silent questioning goes on and on. Their little minds and hearts are struggling, trying desperately to grasp this unthinkable tragedy.

Some go internal. Some act out. Many get angry, temperamental, or moody. Some have dreams of their sibling, or nightmares. Some might take on parts of their deceased sibling's personality, such as their likes and dislikes. Others draw pictures. Children have many ways of remembering their brother or sister and keeping them alive in their hearts.

As parents, we're on grief overload. We yearn for our deceased child, and we hurt for our other kids too. Our hearts are doubly crushed. Parenting right now can feel about as doable as swimming unassisted across an ocean.

Even with other kids in the mix, our focus should still be to grieve responsibly and in a healthy manner. We love our other kids by first taking good care of ourselves. If we don't process our own grief, it will leak out in ways which will not benefit our families.

Part of taking care of ourselves is being honest with our children about what happened, according to their age and ability to understand. We need to express our grief and be real. This hurts. It's confusing. Their sister has died. She is not coming back. We all miss her terribly, but we will get through this together. We all still love her. We will talk about her, share stories about her, and celebrate her life. She is not here with us, but she is still a part of this family.

Kids grieve differently. They grieve over a long period of time, and in spurts. We need to become great listeners and astute observers. We can ask questions, invite them to talk, and draw pictures with them. Their grief will spill forth in snippets, sound bites, sudden tears, and bursts of anger.

Lastly, we're nuts if we think we can do this by ourselves. We need to involve other people who are supportive and know what they're doing. Trusted friends or family can babysit while we get needed breaks. A grief counselor or therapist can provide invaluable assistance on what to do and how. Support groups for us (and for our kids, if available!) put us in contact with others affected by loss.

A child's death impacts the entire family. As much as possible, we need to do this together.

"My other kids are hurting too. We will find ways to grieve together."

AN EXERCISE TO TRY:

This exercise is designed to help you create a simple plan for family grieving. Take some time and think through the following:

What next step can you take in...

...grieving responsibly and in a healthy manner?

...taking care of yourself?

...helping your kids express their own questions and grief?

...involving people who can help your family recover and adjust to this terrible loss?

Someone is missing, and everyone in your family feels it acutely. Keep this in mind. Breathe deeply. One small step at a time.

FROM A FELLOW GRIEVING PARENT:

"Remember, you will feel alone, but you never are. Be open to help. Look for supportive people."

CHAPTER 38

TOXIC PEOPLE: "PEOPLE CAN BE INSENSITIVE AND MEAN"

"I have heard many things like these. You are miserable comforters, all of you."

— The Book of Job

"PEOPLE CAN BE SO INSENSITIVE and mean. Do they realize what they're saying?" Janet said, wringing a napkin in her hands.

Janet's daughter Courtney was a tough and determined survivor. Diagnosed with lymphoma in her late teens, Courtney battled through treatment regimens, kept her spirits up, and dedicated her life to serving others. One Thursday afternoon while she was having lunch with friends, she suddenly lost consciousness and stopped breathing. Courtney was 37.

"Words can cut deep," Janet continued. "Some people mean well, but others can be cruel. I miss Courtney. I always will. How can I not grieve?"

SOME PEOPLE CAN BE TOXIC

The death of a child will powerfully impact our relation-

159

ships. Some people will step up and be helpful. Others will disappear. Still others might be hurtful or demeaning.

Many people are scared, anxious, and living on the emotional edge. Some are surly, angry, and bitter. The pain tends to spill out in what we say. Words can be sharp and cutting, even cruel.

"Are you still grieving? What's wrong with you? Pull it together."

"Life goes on. You should be over this by now."

"I thought you were better and stronger than this."

"People die. It's part of life. You still have other children."

"Isn't she better off now? You should be happy."

We've all heard similar, equally shocking examples we could add to this list. Why do people say these things? Are they afraid of pain? Has our grief triggered unresolved issues from their past? Has our loss unearthed some buried terror? Are they just mean?

It's important to realize that what people say is mostly about them—their emotions, fears, hurts, anger, and pain. People who utter unkind, toxic statements are revealing something about themselves.

Our hearts have been shattered. The last thing we need is someone tromping into our lives and smashing the remaining pieces. We need support, compassion, and hope.

We're back to one of the basic components for healthy grieving: Get around people who are helpful and limit exposure to those who aren't. We don't have time, energy, or space for toxic people. Their voice hinders grieving, recovery, and healing. They are best avoided. If we can't (family members or work associates, for example), we need to devise a survival strategy for when we have to be around them.

How do we respond to the toxic statements of others? One option is to not respond at all. Simply walk away. Unkind statements often don't deserve a response. In most cases, almost anything we say will only become gasoline on a fire. Toxic people are often bitter, angry, and looking for a fight. Firing back at a toxic person usually only leads to being shot at again.

If we feel we must say something, it might be best to come up with a canned response. "Thanks for your concern." "Yes, I'm still grieving. I always will." "I'm working on it."

We can't control the words or actions of toxic people, but we can limit the access they get to our hearts.

"I'll avoid toxic people. My heart and my love for you are too important not to."

AN EXERCISE TO TRY:

List some of the unkind things people have said or done since your child died.

Write a letter or poem to these people (that you will never send), sharing what you think and feel about their actions.

Read the letter out loud, imagining them in front of you.

Take your list of toxic statements. Wad it up in your hand, or tear it into pieces. Throw it in the trash can (or put it through the shredder!). Say out loud, "What people say and do is more about them than it is about me."

Get around people who are helpful to you, and limit your exposure to those who aren't.

FROM A FELLOW GRIEVING PARENT:

"Don't worry or care about what others think of your grief. They haven't been there."

CHAPTER 39

SAFE PEOPLE: "I Can Be Myself with Him"

"Healing is first about finding safety."

— *Tom Golden*

"I don't know what I would do without Steve," Tom said. "He came up to me at the funeral, shook my hand, and looked me in the eye. He didn't say a word. The next week, he sent me a text. Later he called. We got together for coffee. He sat there, and listened."

Garrett was Tom's only son. Tom felt the deep connection the first moment he held Garrett after he was born. As Garrett grew, he and his dad were extremely close.

Garrett was a healthy, athletic kid. After college, he wound up in the ER with an appendicitis. Complications set in. A blood clot ended Garrett's life. He was 23.

"Some days I can barely get out of bed. If I manage to text Steve, I feel better immediately. I can be myself with him," Tom shared.

SAFE PEOPLE MAKE A MASSIVE DIFFERENCE

The people immediately around us have great influence on

our grief process. In the last chapter, we discussed how frustrating toxic people can be and how to handle them. In this chapter, we'll discuss those on the other end of the spectrum — safe people.

What is a safe person?

They don't try to fix. They don't judge or belittle. They don't give advice we haven't asked for. They don't have an agenda for how we should progress. They don't need us to be a certain way. They don't see us as some kind of project. They aren't shocked by emotion or chased away by pain.

They allow us to be ourselves. They accept us where we are, as we are. They listen. And listen.

They seem comfortable with silence. They don't pretend to have answers. They enter our world and exist with us there. Their presence is powerful. Just being with them somehow brings comfort and encouragement to our hearts. They are a bit of sanity in all this craziness. They are solid ground for us in a desert of shifting sand.

Where can we find safe people? Honestly, they could be anywhere, and everywhere. In our family or circle of friends. In churches or civic organizations. In clubs or support groups. They might be mentors, ministers, grief counselors, or therapists. It could be someone we know, or someone we have yet to meet.

We need safe people. It's great if they come knocking on our door, but we can't count on that. We must find them. And the best way to find a safe person is to become one.

Safe people recognize each other. Becoming safe people can greatly enhance our own adjustment and recovery. As we learn to listen without judgment, accept others as they are, and refuse to fix, we liberate ourselves to love others and ourselves. Being a safe person is a part of grieving responsibly and in a healthy manner.

Safe people are positive, healing influences in our lives. Just one can make a life-altering difference.

"I'm not alone. There are others willing to walk this road with me."

QUESTIONS TO CONSIDER:

Who do you know that you would describe as a safe person? What makes them safe?

Do you have regular time with a safe person? If not, are you willing to initiate and ask?

If you don't know a safe person, where do you think you might find one? Can anyone you know help you with this?

FROM A FELLOW GRIEVING PARENT:

"Find people who support you well. Put them on speed dial. Don't try this alone."

CHAPTER 40

NEW SUPPORT: "We've Found Some Kindred Spirits"

> *"Those who have suffered understand suffering and therefore extend their hand."*
>
> — *Patti Smith*

"BEING WITH OTHERS WHO ARE grieving has been important for us. We've found some kindred spirits," Patty said.

"At first I didn't want to go, but I'm glad I did," Bob chimed in. "Most meetings I don't say much. I can't. But being there matters. I'm somehow better afterwards."

Patty and Bob's son Josh was their pride and joy. Their only child, he was lavished with all the love, energy, and attention they could muster. Josh did well, went to college, landed a good job, and got married. They were so proud.

Late one night driving home from a business trip, Josh feel asleep at the wheel. The resulting one-car accident claimed his life. Josh was 29.

"It's an unthinkable nightmare. Honestly, if it wasn't for our support group, we might not be functioning," Patty shared, while Bob nodded in the background.

FINDING OTHERS WHO KNOW
GRIEF IS IMPORTANT

Finding others who know loss can be affirming and comforting. If they've experienced the death of a child, we can look into their eyes and know "they get it." Grief connections like this can be positive and healing.

When a child dies, we're thrown into a forbidding wilderness that seems virtually unpopulated. We're stunned, shattered, and feel very much alone.

Then people start coming forward, or we happen to trip across them here and there. They too have lost a child. We can see grief we understand in their eyes and on their shoulders. Yes, they are in the same club.

Many attempt to hide their grief. They see loss and pain as a private thing. They steel themselves to endure this alone. They don't want to trouble anyone, or perhaps they simply don't trust that anyone will care enough to take them seriously.

Yet we don't have to endure this alone, and we weren't meant to. There are others with similar holes in their hearts, slogging along, stumbling forward. No one can ever fully understand how we feel. But there are those who can do more than sympathize. They can empathize.

Knowing support groups might be a good idea is one thing, but taking the step to call and get info is another. Getting in the car and actually showing up can be, well, terrifying. It seems like we're going to a scary place, back into the darkness of our loss, and we wonder if we can make it through without losing it.

This is a natural concern that can keep us isolated in our grief, and even intensify the process. Those who muster the courage to take the risk and go are usually glad they did. The benefits can be extraordinary.

Saying we know we're not alone is good. Actually discovering and experiencing fellow travelers along this up-and-down grief road can be relieving and comforting.

> *"I'll find other grieving hearts I can connect with. This is another way I can honor you."*

AN EXERCISE TO TRY:

If you haven't already...

- Try to locate a grief support group in your area (The Compassionate Friends, Bereaved Parents, local hospices, churches, grief centers). Consider making contact for more information.

- Consider trying one of these groups. If you're reluctant, see if one of your safe people would be willing to go with you the first time.

- Find an online support group on Facebook or LinkedIn. These people can provide an excellent extra layer of support. You don't need to leave home and can participate according to your schedule.

If you're already attending a support group, consider asking how you might be more involved or serve in the group somehow.

If you've tried a support group and it wasn't that helpful for you, please don't give up on future opportunities. Support groups can be like buying a new pair of shoes. You may have to try one or two before you find one that fits.

FROM A FELLOW GRIEVING PARENT:

"Find a support group you like and can relate well to. Find one that will let you grieve, but also help you work through your grief in positive ways."

CHAPTER 41

COUNSELING: "I DIDN'T THINK IT WOULD HELP"

"There is no grief like the grief that does not speak."

-Henry Wordsworth

"I DIDN'T THINK COUNSELING WOULD help. I was wrong," Charles shared.

Charles' son Jonathan was an independent kid with a strong personality. Somehow, he got through high school unscathed and had a wonderful college career. He worked hard and did well financially. He married, and was blessed with two beautiful kids.

One winter, Jonathan suddenly came down with the flu. He went downhill quickly. He died after several days in the hospital. He was 34.

"Watching our boy's life slip away was awful. I felt so helpless," Charles said. "It took a while, but I realized I couldn't do this alone. So I made the call."

COUNSELING CAN BE A GAME-CHANGER

The loss of a child is devastating, confusing, and debilitating. We need help to stay sane, remain functional, and somehow deal with this nightmare that has descended upon us. Thankfully, there are well-trained people out there who have a heart for this. This loss is so large, so emotionally complicated that it's hard to imagine any of us wouldn't benefit from expert help and guidance. But often, personal pride and stereotypes can get in the way and keep us from the counselor's door.

Think of a counselor as a coach. We've been thrust into a new game we've never played before. We know nothing about this game — not even the rules that govern it. It would make sense to connect with someone who knows the game well and can mentor us.

Counselors don't have all the answers. No human does. And in the case of the loss of a child, there are no emotionally satisfying answers to our deepest questions. Yet, for ourselves we must make sense of this somehow. A counselor-coach can help.

Counseling is not a magic pill. The counselor-coach's job is not to make things better or solve issues. They are not that powerful. The counselor's task is to be a safe person, guiding us as we learn how to process this tragedy and the resulting pain. They coach us in how to grieve in responsible and healthy ways. They listen, ask questions, and help us discover which small step to take next.

There are several types of counselor-coaches out there:

- **Grief counselors** are found in local hospices, grief centers, or perhaps local churches. They deal with grief day-in and day-out, and have specialized experience, training, and education to do so. Grief counselors' services are often free, provided by the organization they are affiliated with.

- **Grief therapists** are licensed professional counselors who specialize in grief recovery. They are licensed in the state they reside in as a mental health professional. Grief therapists charge for their services and expertise, and many are on medical insurance networks.

- **Licensed professional counselors** who are not specifically grief therapists can also be extremely helpful. Their education, training, and licensing are similar to that of grief therapists.

- **Pastoral counselors** are highly trained professionals who deal with grief and loss from a religious and spiritual foundation. Some offer their services for free, courtesy of the local church they are on staff with. Other pastoral counselors have private offices and may charge for their services.

Think back over the incredible impact the death of a child has. Our lives are altered forever. We're deeply shaken and affected in every area — emotionally, mentally, physically, and spiritually. All our relationships are changing. We are changing. One-on-one, individualized time with a trained and experienced grief expert can have extraordinary benefits.

Is one-on-one grief counseling for everyone? No. Some of us have amazing, wonderful support systems well stocked with safe, loving, and supportive people. With enough safety, love, and support, most people do well over time.

Interacting with a counselor-coach can be an affirming, encouraging, and eye-opening experience.

"I'll seek the support I need. I'll take my heart seriously."

QUESTIONS TO CONSIDER:

What are your thoughts and feelings about seeking support from a counselor-coach?

If you're receiving counseling, what has that been like for you? How do you sense you are benefiting?

If you would like to explore counseling and don't know where to go from here, try the following:

- Contact local hospices for their services and recommendations.

- Talk with friends, family, and others for their input on who might be a good fit for you.

- Check with your local church or spiritual affiliation for a recommendation or referral.

- If you have a local grief center, contact them for a recommendation.

Seeking the help we need is not a sign of weakness. Instead, it is a sign of strength, intelligence, and common sense.

FROM A FELLOW GRIEVING PARENT:

*"No parent should outlive their child. Find a
group and get counseling. Don't blame yourself.
Guilt is so prevalent in this journey."*

CHAPTER 42

A RECOVERY TEAM: "THANKS TO THEM, I'LL MAKE IT"

*"What we have once enjoyed deeply we can never lose.
All that we love deeply becomes a part of us."*

— *Helen Keller*

"THANKS TO OTHER PEOPLE, I'LL make it. If it takes a village to raise a child, it takes a team of brave hearts to help someone survive the loss of a child," Marge shared.

Marge's daughter Cassandra was her middle child. She grew up feminine and frilly, with a large dose of spunk under the surface. She married her high school sweetheart and had two girls of her own.

Things went well until cancer struck. The disease process was hard on Cassandra's marriage and family. Her decline was excruciating to watch. She died peacefully in her sleep. She was 38.

"Cancer took my girl's life, but it couldn't steal her heart," Marge said. "This is the hardest thing I've ever been through. I'm glad I'm not alone."

A VARIED SUPPORT SYSTEM IS HELPFUL

None of us are designed to go through grief alone. We need each other. All of us need a support system of the right people. Everyone can benefit from having a good Recovery Team.

We've said before that people make all the difference in our grief process, one way or another. It's healthy and healing to get around people who are helpful to us in our grief process and limit our exposure to those who aren't. Having a good support system can make this a little easier.

Safe people

We all need safe people in our lives. We need people who will accept us where we are and walk with us through this wilderness. We need people with whom we can share our hearts.

Physician

We need a medical doctor we respect and trust. Since grief pounds us physically, most likely some weird symptoms or health concerns will pop up. Having someone in our corner who can help distinguish what needs to be addressed and how can be a relief and a comfort.

Grief professional

The emotional impact of this loss can be devastating. Having a grief counselor or mental health professional we can touch base with is key. We can benefit greatly from the training, experience, and expertise of a specialist who serves people in situations like ours.

Spiritual mentor

Our faith and spiritual life is also impacted. Having a spiritual mentor available during this time is a huge asset.

Whether a minister, pastoral counselor, or someone of deep faith experienced in these matters, they can provide comfort and perspective at a time when we desperately need both.

Fellow grievers

We also need to rub shoulders with people who know grief — especially child loss. We usually find these people in support groups. Some of them, however, find us first. Those who have experienced the death of a child are sometimes naturally drawn to each other.

We need different voices at different times. We need different expertise for difficult and complicated issues. We might not contact some of them very much — maybe even not at all — but knowing that they're there and available is huge.

Having good people waiting in the wings is part of taking care of ourselves during this tumultuous time. Having a varied support system in place can help us with the myriad of changes and adjustments that are taking place. A Recovery Team is one more way we can take our hearts seriously and honor the memory of our child.

"I need a good recovery team. Having good people near me makes a big difference."

AN EXERCISE TO TRY:

Who is on your Recovery Team? List them here. If you don't have these people in place, write down who might fill these roles.

- Safe people
- Medical doctor

- Grief counselor or mental health professional
- Spiritual mentor
- People who know grief (esp. child loss)

Are there any of these you need to reach out to presently? If so, make a plan to do that.

Some have a good support system in place. Others have to build one. We are all in unique situations. We start where we are and move forward, one small step at a time.

FROM A FELLOW GRIEVING PARENT:

"You need different kinds of support from different people. Be on the lookout. Those people are probably already there."

WHERE WE'VE BEEN AND WHERE WE'RE GOING...

The death of a child is similar to a nuclear weapon detonating in our lives. Much is annihilated, seemingly vaporized, while other damage has yet to be seen or calculated. How do we survive, much less heal?

Much of the change will be relational. In this section, we discussed the profound impact the loss of a child can have on relationships. We talked about the scope and depth of these changes, and how to make wise and healthy choices in this area.

What people do and say is more about them than about us and our loss. We take care of ourselves better when get around those who are helpful to us and limit our exposure to those who aren't.

Our world has changed. We have changed. Our relationships will change as well.

In the next section, we'll be looking at the future impact of our loss. When someone dies, many of the dreams we had (if not all of them) die as well. Not only the present, but our future has been altered forever.

PART SIX:

FUTURE IMPACT

IN THE PREVIOUS SECTIONS, WE'VE looked at how this tragic loss has impacted our hearts, minds, bodies, souls, and relationships. Our whole being might feel shattered and fragmented.

Yes, our child was that important. Yes, the loss was that great.

We loved them. We love them still. No wonder we hurt and feel so broken.

In this section, we'll discuss how this loss has impacted our future. Because our worlds have changed, our future has too. Fear and foreboding can hijack our hearts. At times, hope can seem to almost disappear.

The past doesn't determine the future, but it significantly influences it. How we look at this loss and process our grief will have a massive impact — on our own lives and those closest to us.

How do we think about the future now? Will this ever get any better? Is it possible to find hope again?

Read on...

CHAPTER 43

IDENTITY CRISIS: "Who am I now?"

"I will never forget the moment when your heart stopped and mine kept beating."

— Angela Miller

"I'M NOT THE SAME PERSON. Neither is Dave. Who am I now? Who are we?" asked Alexandra.

Alexandra and Dave's son Duke was their only child. He was a talkative kid, with an active imagination. He was the superhero of the neighborhood, with a strong preference for Batman and Thor.

Despite watchful and involved parents, Duke began to run with a questionable crowd. In high school, he got into drugs. He pursued some college, but never followed through consistently. He had trouble holding down a job. One morning, Duke's roommate found him unconscious on the floor. His death was ruled an accidental overdose. Duke was 25.

"Duke's death was complicated. So is our grief. I miss him. I miss me. I miss our family," Alexandra shared.

LOSS CAN CREATE AN IDENTITY CRISIS

The loss of a child strikes us at the core of our beings. Part of us has been suddenly, perhaps forcefully, stolen away. Where did they go?

Their absence changes everything—every dynamic, every relationship. Their death hits our hearts and souls. We feel ourselves changing. The person we were, along with the life and family we knew, has been altered forever. Who are we now?

This tragedy had thrown us into an identity crisis. Part of us has disappeared. What do we do with that?

Like waves on a beach, the unwanted changes keep rolling in, continual and relentless. The after-shocks pound us. Collateral damage piles up. Who knew so many little deaths could come from one big one?

The death of a child is an unwanted, painful gift that keeps on giving.

Our hearts are stunned. We're reeling. It feels like we're in a free fall with no safety net. We brace ourselves and wonder what will happen next. We go into fortress-mode, trying desperately to control the damage and protect who and what we have left.

We sense our hearts and lives changing, shifting. We hold our breath, hoping that all this will soon stop and be over somehow. We have dreams about the way things were.

We gaze into the mirror. Who is that? We look different. We are different. Perhaps we barely recognize ourselves.

This identity crisis is a natural and common experience for those suffering the loss of a child. Weathering this storm takes guts. We're in uncharted waters with almost no idea where this violent wind might drive us.

In most cases, this identity crisis will be temporary. As we process the grief, we will adapt, adjust, heal, and grow (though any and all of these might seem impossible on any given day). But we will not go back to who we were. That's impossible. We walk now with a pronounced limp. Every step reminds us of the shattering blow we've experienced.

Who are we? Who will we be? We don't know. But we're not the same, and we won't be.

"I don't know who I am or who I'll become, but I'll never be the same. I don't want to be."

AN EXERCISE TO TRY:

Write a letter to yourself. Describe how you feel about you now, with all the changes that have happened and are still occurring. You can use these writing prompts:

- I'm not who I was. I see this when...

- Since my child's death, here's how I sense I've changed:

- Here's what I miss about myself, my mate, and our family since the death of our child:

When you've finished writing, read the letter out loud in front of a mirror.

How did this exercise affect you?

FROM A FELLOW GRIEVING PARENT:

"My son died 18 years ago. Largely because of him I have now been a hospice chaplain for 14 years. Not exactly what I might have chosen, but a gift from him nonetheless."

CHAPTER 44

PURPOSE: "EVERYTHING FEELS MEANINGLESS"

"We must embrace pain and burn it as fuel for our journey."

— *Kenji Miyazawa*

"I WANDER. I DRIFT. I have no purpose. Everything feels meaningless," Mark said.

"Me too. I'm just here. That's all," Melanie added.

Mark and Melanie's daughter Faith was their third child. After two normal, healthy pregnancies and deliveries, Faith's entry into the world was complicated. She was born with a rare syndrome and was immediately transferred to another hospital for specialized treatment.

Faith did not improve. After several weeks, it was deemed best to remove her from life support. She was 25 days old.

"When her heart stopped, mine stopped too. I have a family, a good life, and a good marriage, yet I wonder why I'm here," Melanie said.

LOSS SHAKES OUR SENSE OF PURPOSE AND MEANING

The death of a child reaches the inmost part of our hearts

and souls. We wonder who we are now, and why we're here. Our sense of identity and purpose can be hard hit.

Life changed the moment our child took their last breath. When their heart stopped beating, something happened to ours too. Nothing would be the same, especially us.

This terrible loss can deeply disturb our sense of purpose. Big losses call many things into question. Our view of life, ourselves, God, and everything else gets hauled before our internal review board. Our wonderings multiply.

How could this happen? What now? Who am I? Why am I here?

In grief, many can feel like a small, lifeless twig, floating swiftly downstream in a rocky river. We get banged up. We're exhausted. We feel powerless, swept along by this irresistible current we have no say in and no control over.

Yet, there is a sense in which we can use the swift current of our grief to honor our child and help ourselves adjust and recover. Part of this includes recovering, redefining, or discovering (perhaps for the first time) our purpose.

Nothing can bring perspective to life like death. We knew that none of us is promised tomorrow. Now we have experienced this hard truth. We see people, life, and events more clearly. We have new eyes. We now know anything can happen to anyone at any time.

This can either crush us, or spur us on to make the most of every day, even each moment. The stakes are high. How we live and respond to this loss matters deeply—not just for ourselves, but for all those around us. Living well in the midst of all this will demand a clear sense of purpose.

Parent, spouse, daughter, son, brother, sister, aunt, uncle, or grandparent. Doctor, lawyer, insurance agent, homemaker, nurse, teacher, cashier, construction specialist, customer service associate, dentist, etc. These are roles we occupy. Crucial, important roles. The problem with roles is that they change. Something happens, and the role can be taken from us.

Our purpose must be bigger than any role we have — even larger than all our roles put together. Our purpose is what drives what we do (our roles) and how we do them.

Is our purpose to serve others? Love others? Treat others as we would have them treat us? Make a positive impact in the world?

What do we want to leave behind? What kind of legacy do we want to shower upon those we love and care about?

Whatever we decide our purpose is, it will include every role we have, and yet transcend them all. It is the driving force behind our relationships, families, jobs, and careers. The more connected our lives are under one single purpose, the more focused, intentional, and meaningful life becomes.

With a clear sense of purpose, decision-making gets easier. Does this fit with who we are and why we're here? Does it help us live out our mission? If multiple options are available, which one is more in line with our purpose?

Our children are tremendously important. Even through their death, they teach us about life. Our child can assist us in discovering and defining our life's purpose. This is part of their legacy to us. We can use our grief to honor them by living more intentionally than ever.

> *"I'll honor my child by living the most meaning-ful life I can. I'll live with purpose."*

QUESTIONS TO CONSIDER:

What has your child taught you about life and relationships?

If someone were to ask you what your purpose in life is, what would you say?

Can this purpose / mission encompass all your roles in life, and yet still be larger than all of them? If not, do you want to redefine or sharpen your purpose in any way?

Is your purpose / mission simple and clear enough to be used to gauge your decisions (relational, financial, educational, familial, etc.)?

We honor our children when we live with purpose.

FROM A FELLOW GRIEVING PARENT:

"Help someone else who has lost a child. Be a shoulder or an ear for another grieving parent. You can make more of a difference than you realize."

CHAPTER 45

MEMORIALS: "I Can Almost See Him Smiling"

"And love is stronger than fear, life stronger than death, hope stronger than despair."

— *Henri Nouwen*

"FOR A WHILE, WE TRIED to forget. That was impossible. So we chose to deliberately remember and tell his story to whomever would listen," Amanda shared.

Amanda and Garland's son Boyd was their middle child. He fell in love with hockey at age four. The game became his obsession. By the time he was 16, his skills on the ice were impressive.

One night, Boyd and three teammates were on their way home from practice and hit a large patch of black ice. The resulting head-on collision killed all but one of the boys and the other driver. Boyd was 18.

"Boyd's coach asked about doing a memorial game to honor the boys and raise teen driving safety awareness. We agreed. It was a huge hit. The next year, it was even bigger and better. Last month, we had the 5th annual memorial game. It's the biggest event in the city now. And traffic fatalities are way down the last three years," Garland said.

"I can almost see Boyd smiling in heaven," Amanda added.

MEMORIALS CAN BE POWERFUL, AND HEALING

We will always remember. And we can use these memories to honor our child, help our families grieve in a healthy manner, and even impact a community for good.

How? By initiating memorials.

Memorials can be almost anything. They are usually built off the personality and passions of our child. If they were an infant or toddler, the memorial can come from what we as parents hoped for them.

Here are some memorials parents have chosen to honor their child and impact lives:

- Annual memorial soccer game followed by hot dog cookout.
- Make a quilt honoring your child and display it.
- Annual teen driving safety assembly at the local high school.
- Paint a rock in memory of your child. Use acrylic paint and spray with clear sealer. Put it in your garden, use as a doorstop, or place beside your child's monument.
- Give a tree in memory of your child to a local park or charity.
- Tennis tournament and drug awareness program
- Have a party with friends at a paint-it-yourself business. Ask people to donate a few extra dollars for a charity gift in your child's honor.

- Memorial baseball game with a brief suicide-prevention program
- Memorial water-bottle giveaway on a hot summer day in a prominent location
- Memory walk to raise funds for charity
- Have an artist friend draw or paint a portrait of your child from a picture, or try it yourself.
- Memorial community cookout and fireworks show
- Community pizza party with alcohol safety awareness program

You get the idea.

Not only are we remembering our child and celebrating their life, but we're also modeling healthy, positive grieving to a world that can be clueless. Our memorials — our children — can have more impact than we realize.

We keep our child's memory out there. We're not afraid to speak their name, and no one else should be either. We shout it out, and invite others to celebrate them with us.

Yes, these events will bring tears. They should. We miss our child. We'll always grieve on some level, but we can use our grief to honor them too, all while making a difference in the lives of others.

Our child mattered. They still do, and always will. Memorials give us a target, a focused avenue to express our love. Lives will be changed for the better because of them.

"I'll find memorials that will honor you and bring a smile to your face. I love you."

AN EXERCISE TO TRY:

Begin to plan a memorial in honor of your child. The following questions can help.

If your child was old enough, what were their passions and interests? (If they were an infant or toddler, what are your passions and interests?)

Brainstorm some possibilities of memorials based on these passions and interests. Don't censor them yet based on what you think is possible. Just brainstorm possibilities.

Of these possibilities, which one does your heart resonate with the most?

How might you go about making this memorial a reality? Who and what would you need? List them here.

What's your next step?

Memorials are expressions of love for our child and for those around us.

FROM A FELLOW GRIEVING PARENT:

*"Your child's life counted, and counts still.
Celebrate them any way you can!"*

CHAPTER 46

HOLIDAYS: "CAN'T WE JUST SKIP THE HOLIDAYS?"

"The past does not haunt us. We haunt the past."

— *Augusten Burroughs*

"CHRISTMAS? THANKSGIVING WAS AN EMOTIONAL nightmare. Can't we just skip it this year? Where's the Grinch when you need him?" Glenn asked.

"I'm planning on hiding. I know it won't work, but I don't know what else to do," Connie added.

Glenn and Connie's daughter Skylar grew up into a beautiful and rugged young lady. Her two brothers proudly took credit for the rugged part. Together they loved hunting, fishing, and the outdoors.

One summer vacation, the family camped at a gorgeous spot next to a river. Early one morning, during a tubing excursion down the river, Skylar's younger brother fell in and went under. Without hesitation, she went after him. As she tugged him to safety, Skylar was knocked unconscious. She slipped away quickly, as her brothers watched in horror. She was 15.

"She's our hero. How do we do Christmas, or any holiday for that matter, without her?" Glenn asked.

HOLIDAYS CAN BE TOUGH

Thanksgiving. Christmas. New Year's. Valentines. Memorial Day. July 4. Labor Day. These are the times when families gather to enjoy one another and celebrate. For those of us enduring loss, these days are often devoured by the absence of our loved one.

Holidays are tough. They surface our losses in ways nothing else can, especially Thanksgiving and Christmas. Far from a celebration, these times seem more like some cruel joke. Surrounded by festive atmosphere, sparkling lights, and holiday décor, we sigh and weep. Holiday cheer is replaced by holiday sadness. We've lost a child, and the reminders are everywhere. We bump into a memory with every step.

What do we do with this? Some of us opt for hiding. We emotionally, and sometimes physically, lock ourselves in, hunker down, and wait for the present storm to pass. The sheer dread of the assault of memories can be paralyzing.

Yet, the holiday comes. Is it possible to meet it and somehow use it to honor our child and express our grief in a healthy way?

Yes, but it's going to take some intentional, proactive thinking and decision-making.

Let's consider for a moment. What about this holiday reminds us of our child? What fond memories does this time of year evoke? Is there something our child especially enjoyed? What are some of our favorite memories of them during this time? Is there are way to use this holiday to remember and honor them?

Here are some examples from other parents:

- Put a stocking up for them. Have everyone bring a card that reminds them of that child and put it in the stocking. Pass around the cards on Christmas Eve or morning, and read them out loud.

- Wrap an empty box and put it under the tree, with the child's name on it. When presents are opened, pass it around and have each person share a memory.

- As a family, light a candle in remembrance, and share some memories.

- Have each family member write a brief letter or poem to your child. Read them out loud together at some point during the holiday.

- Enlarge a picture of your child. Provide markers and have family members or friends write messages on the picture. Display it during the holidays.

- Prepare a favorite dish of your child and include it in the holiday meal.

- During the holiday meal, take some time and focus on your child. Have those present share a memory.

- Do something completely new, like take a trip somewhere you've never been, and honor your child in some way during your time together as a family.

These are just a few examples. The key is being creative and proactive. We need a plan—even a simple one. In fact, simple is probably best.

Many are concerned activities like these will be too emotional and infuse the holidays with sadness. The truth is, things are already emotional. When families get together, everyone is hyper-aware of who's missing. Having a plan to honor our child gives our families an opportunity to share and grieve together in a healthy way.

Yes, it will be emotional, but that's doesn't mean it can't be good.

The holiday will come. Be proactive. Be creative. Make a plan. Keep it simple.

We don't have to let the holidays crush us. Rather, with a little proactive decision-making we can use this time to express our grief in a healthy manner, honor our child, and love those around us.

"The holidays are coming. I will meet them head-on, and use them to honor you."

AN EXERCISE TO TRY:

What's the next holiday you're concerned about?

Brainstorm some simple activities you could do to honor your child this holiday. Don't evaluate them, but let the ideas flow.

Choose one of these. Make a plan. What and who do you need to pull this off?

Watch out for the expectations of others. You get to choose what to do, how, when, and with whom. Take care of yourself. Honor your child's memory and celebrate their life.

You can use this holiday, instead of letting the holiday use you.

FROM A FELLOW GRIEVING PARENT:

"You're learning to live with a large piece of yourself gone – and that includes holidays. Breathe. Be patient. Be kind. Hang on."

CHAPTER 47

BIRTHDAYS AND ANNIVERSARIES:
"Certain Days are Hard!"

"Those we love never truly leave us, Harry.
There are things that death cannot touch."

— J.K. Rowling

"Certain days are hard, and always will be. His birthday is one. The anniversary of his death is another," Marleen said.

Marleen's son Jacob was born with muscular dystrophy, but he never thought of himself as handicapped. He was a smiling, engaging, well-liked, and happy kid.

One day Jacob fell and broke his leg. During his hospital stay, sepsis set in. He was gone in less than a day. Jacob was nine years old.

"I miss him. I long for him every day. His death is easily the greatest wound of my life," Marlene shared.

SPECIAL DAYS CAN BE CHALLENGING

When we lose a child, certain days of the year automatically become challenging. Birthdays and death anniversaries are two of the toughest.

Birthdays are designed to celebrate another year of life. Our child's birthday is a reminder of another year without them. Anniversaries typically mark special occasions, but when our child's death-date rolls around, it can launch us back into acute, intense grief. These special days bring it all back. The pain can be incredible.

As with Thanksgiving, Christmas, and other holidays, these spaces on the calendar will not disappear. Even if we wanted to avoid them, we couldn't. Certain days are etched deep into our souls. They will not be blocked out, erased, or forgotten.

Since birthdays and anniversaries will come, we must deal with them. They are part of the aftermath of our loss. They remind us of what was and is no longer. Along with other aspects of this loss, we must find ways to use them to love and honor our child.

Here is the shift we need to make: Begin to view these days as times of remembrance and opportunities to celebrate the life of our child and tell their story. It's a simple shift, but not an easy one.

It's okay if these days are painful. They should be. It's natural if we experience a sense of dread as their birthday or anniversary approaches. We love and miss them. This hurts.

How can we use birthdays and anniversaries in a positive and healthy way? Here are some possibilities:

- Have a birthday party and invite family, friends, neighbors, and our child's friends.
- Have a short time of remembrance. Light a candle. Release balloons, butterflies, or a dove or pigeon.
- Host a letter-writing party. Everyone writes a letter to your child, and then someone other than the person who wrote it reads it out loud.

- Host a card party. Everyone brings a card for your child, and explains why they chose the card they did.

- Take your family and serve that day in honor of your child (soup kitchen, hospital, church, school, etc.)

- Have a meal with some of your child's favorite foods. Have everyone there share a memory.

- Have an art session where everyone draws something that reminds them of your child. Have them share why they drew what they did.

- Organize a memory walk for charity. Share stories of your child throughout the walk.

And that's just the beginning. There are many possibilities, many ways we could use these days for good. If your child was born or died on a major holiday, don't feel like you have to do what others are doing on that day. Make the day work for you, your family, your child, and your grief.

Our child's birthday is worth celebrating. Honoring them on the anniversary of their death is fitting and healing. How we view, approach, and use these special times matters.

"I can honor you on your birthday and the day of your death. I'll work on this."

AN EXERCISE TO TRY:

Choose one: your child's birthday or the anniversary of their death.

Take a few moments and brainstorm some ways you could

celebrate and honor them that day. For now, don't worry about what's realistic. Dream a little.

Of the possibilities you brainstormed, which one does your heart resonate with the most?

What and who do you need to pull this idea off?

What's your next step?

Be proactive. Be creative. Make a plan. Keep it simple.

FROM A FELLOW GRIEVING PARENT:

*"Special days won't ever be easy again,
but you can make them good."*

CHAPTER 48

HELPING SIBLINGS: "How do
we help the other kids?"

---

*"The reason it hurts so much to separate is
because our souls are connected."*

— Nicholas Sparks

"WE WANT TO HELP THE other kids through this, but we
don't have a clue what to do or say," Thomas said.

"We know they're hurting. How do we do this?" Marta
asked.

Marta and Thomas' son Karl was the oldest of four kids.
He was energetic, and a natural leader. His siblings looked
up to him.

Karl was the commander in chief of the kids' tree
house. One Saturday afternoon, Karl's little sister lost her
footing. Karl leaped forward, grabbed her shirt, and pulled
her back to safety. The resulting force catapulted Karl out
of the tree house, head first. He never regained consciousness. He was 12 years old.

"His little brother sometimes cries out for Karl in his
sleep. This is truly awful," Marta said.

HELPING OUR OTHERS KIDS WHILE
GRIEVING OURSELVES

Losing a sibling growing up is a painful and traumatic experience. Even as adults, the death of a brother or sister cuts deep. As parents, if we have other kids still at home, we're naturally concerned for their welfare during this time.

This can be overwhelming. We force ourselves up, trying to be functional for the sake of our kids. We steel ourselves to be as stable and strong as possible.

Strong? How do we do that when we're crushed? What does strong even mean in this situation?

Stable? Our hearts have been shattered. At best, we're tottering.

What do we do?

We grieve.

We express our grief in a way that fits us, in the healthiest way possible. And yes, we grieve openly, in front of our kids (not all our grief, of course). It's helpful for them to see us be sad, tear up, and cry. If it's okay for us to grieve, their little hearts assume that it's okay for them to hurt, be sad, and cry too. We can simply grieve, and let them join us.

We can talk openly about what we miss. We can ask our kids what they miss. We can share the questions we have and ask them what's on their mind and what they're wondering about.

Here are some possibilities:

- Put a feeling emoji sheet on the fridge and a magnet for each person. Have each person move their magnet around the sheet during the day depending on how they're feeling.

- Ask them what questions they have about their sibling, or about death.

- Draw pictures with them while talking about what they're thinking and feeling.

- Watch one of your child's favorite movies. After the movie, take some time for each person to share a memory.

- Have a meal with some of your child's favorite foods. Use this as a time to talk about him or her.

- Consider having a short, regular, personal time with each child. Share together about what you miss most that day.

- Go to grief counseling together as a family — or with one child at a time.

- Look for grief support for children at hospices, grief centers, or local churches.

Be creative. Keep it simple. No matter what we do to help our kids grieve, we can focus on:

- Being ourselves
- Being loving
- Expressing our grief in healthy ways
- Assuring them it's okay to hurt, cry, and miss their sibling
- Fostering an environment where their questions are welcomed and heard

Be with them. Share with them. Be available.

If you lost an adult child and your children are older, a lot of the dynamics and situations will be different, but the basic principles are the same. Take care of yourself. Grieve in a healthy and responsible way. Express your grief openly in front of your children. Invite them to grieve with you.

> *"Your siblings are hurting too. We're a family. We all grieve for you."*

AN EXERCISE TO TRY:

How can you help your other kids grieve? Here are some thoughts to work through:

How can you model for your kids what it means to grieve in healthy ways?

Brainstorm some way you can connect with your kids and help them process their grief during this time. Perhaps consider some of the bullet point suggestions on the previous page.

Which one of these would you like to start with?

Don't expect to get this right. There is no right or perfect here. Focus on being loving and connecting with your kids. If you do that, you can't lose.

FROM A FELLOW GRIEVING PARENT:

> *"One thing at a time. One step at a time. One moment at a time. One second at a time."*

CHAPTER 49

ENDURANCE: "Does It Ever Get Any Better?"

"Grief, a type of sadness that most often occurs
when you have lost someone you love,
is a sneaky thing, because it can disappear for a long time,
and then pop back up when you least expect it."

— *Lemony Snicket*

"Does it ever get any better? Everyone says I should be over this or further along." Annette said.

Annette's daughter Kimberly was the younger of two girls. She loved pink, dogs, and horses. If she had the option, she would have lived outside. She did well in school, and then worked her way through college as a veterinary tech.

On the way home from her college graduation with some friends, a truck crossed the median and slammed into them head-on. The truck driver was the only survivor. Kimberly was 23.

"I never got to say goodbye. How do I recover from that?" Annette asked.

GRIEF HAS NO TIMETABLE

The power and depth of this loss is staggering. We get hit on every level, every day. We discover more losses as we go. Weeks become months, and months become years. We wince. We ache. Our hearts are shattered. How long is this supposed to go on?

There is no "supposed to" when it comes to the intensity and duration of our grief. Every person, every relationship, and every loss is different. Our grief process is influenced by a variety of factors:

- Who we are – our personality and internal resources
- Our personal history of loss – other losses we've experienced and how they've affected us
- Our personal relationship with our child – the depth and kind of our attachment
- The child themselves – personality, age, station in life, etc.
- The nature of the death – illness, accident, violent death, etc.
- Our physical and mental health
- Our faith and spiritual condition – what we believe about life, death, the afterlife
- The kind and degree of other current stressors (relational, financial, vocational, physical, etc.)

As a result of all these factors, there are no exact time lines for the progression of our grief. There are no infallible standards for what we "should" be experiencing and when. There are only patterns, and these vary greatly depending on the nature and depth of the factors listed above.

No matter what our situation, as we process our grief in

healthy ways, the intensity of our emotions will most likely lessen. As time goes on our loss settles in at new levels. Moments of shock and denial recede and diminish, giving way to a dull and heavy awareness of reality. As our hearts begin to adjust to this terrible loss, the grief isn't necessarily better or easier, but different.

As we grieve, our children get assimilated into our lives in new ways. We don't move on without them or leave them behind. They become even more a part of us. We heal, but we're not the same. We learn to live with a hole in our hearts.

On some level, we will never stop grieving. We will always miss them. We will never forget. But our grief will change. Time does not heal all wounds, but healing and recovery do take time.

Our hearts refuse to be on a grief time schedule. Grief is not a task to be performed or an item to check off a to-do list. It's a dynamic, variable, personal, and somewhat unpredictable process. We grieve because we dared to love.

"My grief has no time limit. I'll always
grieve, but it will change over time."

SOME QUESTIONS TO CONSIDER:

Have other people implied (or have you thought) that you should be "further along," "over this by now," or "better?" Has this expectation helped you?

Have you sensed your grief changing over time? How so?

What are some of your greatest struggles at present?

Wanting to feel better is natural and common. None of us wants or likes pain. As we process it in healthy ways, the grief will change over time. We will adjust to this loss, and live honoring our child and their memory.

FROM A FELLOW GRIEVING PARENT:

"Your grief is yours. There is no timeline or time limit. Give yourself time to grieve."

CHAPTER 50

FINDING HOPE: "I'll Learn to Live Again"

"Grief never ends...but it changes."

— *Unknown*

"I'll always grieve, but I'll somehow learn to live again," Will said.

Will's son Adam had a complicated childhood. His mom left when he was three. He didn't remember her, but he never got over it.

Though Will did a marvelous job as a single parent, Adam struggled. His angst and depression led him to drugs. Eventually, Adam took his own life. He was 17.

"The pain was terrible. People got me through it — great friends, a support group, a counselor, and a doctor," Will shared. "I began to breathe again. Adam has become more a part of me than ever. I love him. I always will."

FINDING HOPE AGAIN

Finding hope is crucial. With the loss of a child, it can seem to disappear. Our hearts are so wounded that we can't even imagine it. Healing in any shape, form, or fashion seems impossible.

As we move through our grief, things begin to change over time. Our hearts begin to beat again. Our souls slowly wake, as if from a coma. Color gradually returns to the dull, gray world we've been living in.

And one day we sense something we haven't felt for a long time. Hope.

The truth is that hope didn't take a hiatus. It's always been there, but our shattered hearts couldn't see it, much less take it in. As we process our grief in responsible and healthy ways, more space opens up in our pain-riddled hearts. We sense hope's presence again.

Our child has become more a part of us. They have settled into their always-place in our hearts, though they are no longer physically present in our daily lives. Hope, like a gentle breeze on a stagnant day, begins to blow through our souls again.

And suddenly we realize an important fact: we're going to make it. We're going to survive this. We will live on, honoring and loving our child along the way.

Granted, at any given moment we may not feel hopeful at all. Many of us are still in the heat of the emotional battle, bouncing from sadness to anger to fear to anxiety to depression and back again. We may feel forlorn and empty. Exhaustion might be the current state of our existence. But it will not always be so.

Grief is a long and winding road. It meanders over many hills and through multiple valleys. As we travel, the landscape is forever changing, as do the people around us and our circumstances. We trudge on, one small step at a time, leaning forward as best we can. It is a journey through uncharted territory.

Eventually, calmer terrain greets us. The sun shines a bit more. The air grows lighter, fresher. Even some flowers begin to appear along the side of the road.

We carry our child with us, inside us, to greet the next portion of the journey. Which way the road will turn, we don't know. But we do know we love our children, and that we will live to honor them any way we can. We will walk on, telling their story, for it is our story too.

Love endures. It always has. It always will.

"Hope will return. I believe this. I love you. I always will."

SOME QUESTIONS TO CONSIDER:

Can you see any hope in your daily life at present? If so, where? If not, begin to look for it and see what you notice.

Will mentioned that he was getting through this time because of the people in his life (safe people, friends, a support group, a counselor, and a doctor). Is there anyone you need to reach out to and spend time with? What's the next step?

If you could change anything about your daily life (except for having your child back, of course), what would it be? Is there a step you can take toward this change?

Hope is always there. Sometimes, we simply don't have eyes to see it. Hope is never dependent on us. It waits, and blesses us when we're ready.

FROM A FELLOW GRIEVING PARENT:

"If you focus on remembering and sharing your child with others, you will survive. You will even do well, and learn to live again."

WHERE WE'VE BEEN AND WHERE WE'RE GOING...

In this section, we discussed the impact the loss of a child can have on our future. Their death can throw us into an identity crisis and cause us to question our purpose in life. We may have to rediscover who we are and why we're here.

Finding memorials and using holidays well can assist us in our grief process. Having realistic expectations of ourselves, and others, is important to our health and wellbeing as we grieve. Our grief has no time limit. It is not an item to be checked off a list, or a task to be accomplished.

We may always grieve. Certainly, we will always miss our child. But as we recover and heal, the grief we experience will change. We loved our child, and we love them still. We can find ways to live that out, honor them, and love those around us as well.

This is hard. It's not for sissies. You have far more courage than you realize.

Breathe deeply. You can be courageous again today—one tiny step at a time.

CONCLUDING THOUGHTS:

A Personal Perspective on Grief and Loss

"Mourn with those who mourn."

— The Apostle Paul

"Jesus wept."

— John 11:35

THANK YOU FOR TAKING YOUR heart seriously and reading this book. I hope you found it comforting and helpful. Most of all, I trust you know you're not alone. Our losses are all unique, which makes grief a lonely road. But we can still walk it together.

I wanted to conclude by sharing my personal perspective on grief, loss, and healing. I do this hoping that somehow my thoughts and experience might be beneficial to you in your journey through this emotional, mental, physical, and spiritual minefield.

I AM A FELLOW STRUGGLER

As I mentioned in the introductory chapter, I am a fellow struggler. I have not arrived. I haven't figured this grief thing out. I tussle daily with issues stemming from the losses I have endured and continue to face. I trip and stumble a lot in life, but hopefully I'm falling forward along the way.

I am a Christian, a follower of Jesus Christ. I'm inconsistent, far from perfect, and downright weak at times. I'm often confused, frustrated, and more anxious than I would like to admit. I am a walking, breathing mass of contradictions. But Jesus is my life, and this influences what I think, do, and say — and how I write.

If you come from a different faith orientation or perhaps claim no particular faith at all, my goal here is not to offend you or cause you distress. Far from it. My purpose is to share what has been personally helpful to me in navigating this up-and-down existence of multiple losses in the hope that it will be beneficial to you as well.

So please take the following for what it is — my story. I'm not saying that it should be yours. Your story is your own.

MY EARLY STORY

I lost both grandfathers very early. Honestly, I hardly remember anything about either one of them. Due to dementia, one grandmother never knew who I was. Though I had many relatives nearby, my nuclear family was isolated and relationally distant from them. I remember feeling sad and lonely most of the time.

I lost large chunks of early childhood to repetitive and traumatic sexual abuse. This greatly shaped my view of myself, others, the world, and God. My sadness and loneliness grew. I went internal. During this time my brother, who was already in college, lost a girlfriend in a car accident and another friend in Vietnam. I remember the atmosphere of grief that permeated our home. It was stifling and had a tinge of hopelessness to it.

When I was 12, a good school buddy died suddenly of spinal meningitis over the Christmas holidays. He sat right in front of me in homeroom. Every morning for the rest of the year, I came in and stared at his empty desk. He was so bright, fun, full of promise, and healthy. How could things like this happen?

My parents' marriage was not a peaceful one. Yelling and screaming were common. They finally separated and divorced in my early teens. By default, I stayed with Mom. She had serious, ongoing mental health issues, which no one seemed to know what to do with. She slipped deeper and deeper into a world of grandiose delusions. It was not a good situation. I moved in with Dad.

The next six months were some of the best of my life. I was 15, and felt like I was finally getting my feet under me. Dad was stable, and his presence provided a strong sense of safety. Then one Sunday afternoon, he collapsed in front of me of a massive heart attack. He never regained consciousness, and died a week later. My world, as I knew it, was over.

Reluctantly, I moved back in with Mom, who was even more unstable than before. Several months later, she attempted to take her own life. As she went into psychiatric care in the local hospital, it struck me that for all practical purposes I was an orphan.

As you know, not all losses are deaths. And a death is not simply one loss either. Every loss, every death, has other losses, other little deaths, attached to it. Collateral damage. The losses pile up. My collateral damage was at such a point that my recollection of this time is garbled. I have memory gaps. Grief does that to us.

Life was not at all what I thought or hoped it would be. It was full of surprises, most of which were unwelcome and painful. I can see myself sitting on the couch in that lonely, empty apartment, wondering where the next hit was going to come from.

Then something deep within me began to surface. A resolve. Something in my heart was tired of all this. I wanted to fight.

In my simple, teenage way I accepted reality. Life was going to be hard. Bad stuff was going to happen. I was not in control of this. I did not have much say (if any) in what happened to me or around me. I could only control my responses.

At that point, I made two decisions. First, I resolved to bring as little distress on myself as possible. In other words, keep my nose clean, live well, and create as few disasters as I could. Second, I resolved to face grief and loss head-on, to fight, and to heal. Abuse, death, and collateral damage would not win.

About this time, I was taken in by the family of my best friend. They already had four kids, and adding an at-risk kid like me to the mix was potentially dangerous. But they did it anyway.

I can recall the day my mom dropped me at their front door with a couple of suitcases. "Here you go," she said to them, and drove off. I sighed and walked into their home. Twin emotions gripped me — deep sadness, along with a profound, powerful feeling of safety.

They loved me as their own son. They accepted and supported me in every way possible. I went through the days pinching myself, wondering if this could possibly be real. It was so good, in fact, that I simply couldn't take it all in.

One afternoon, I entered the dad's office and sat down in front of his desk. I asked why in the world he would take in a kid like me and make me a part of his family. He smiled, leaned forward, and said, "Gary, with what Jesus Christ did for us, how could we not do this for you?"

Something clicked in my heart. Jesus was not new to me. I began going to church when I was ten. I was hurting and looking for hope. I got to know Jesus there. However, I wasn't interested in religion. I needed love and relationship.

Now, here he was again, this Jesus.

I walked out of my new dad's office that day with a new sense of meaning and purpose. I launched on a lifelong journey to heal from the past. It was time to live a different life.

AN ADVENTURE OF HEALING

I went to college and studied Psychology (surprise!). I immersed myself in service, and found myself continually surrounded by troubled, grieving, and wounded people. People like me. Ever since, my adult life has been dedicated to helping hurting people heal and grow, finding greater perspective and healing for myself along the way.

As I got older, the losses continued to pile up, as they do with all of us. In addition, as a missionary and pastor, I was frequently around pain, grief, and loss. Now as a hospice chaplain and grief counselor, I'm in the presence of death every day. Grief is part of the air I breathe. So many are hurting. Different people with diverse backgrounds, unique relationships, deeply personal losses, and different faiths.

But we all have this in common: we are human, and we experience loss.

I believe God knows our pain. More than this, I believe he feels it.

I believe he created us in his image, which means we're all of priceless, eternal value. We're designed for relationship, to love and be loved. We don't do separation well. Our hearts break and shatter. God knows this. He walks with us in the valley of the shadow of death, though many times we are unaware of his presence.

Then there is this Jesus character. The Bible declares him to be God who has taken on human flesh. He came among us, walked with us, and experienced the joy, delight, and love that quality relationships can bring. He also tasted the ugliness of injustice, deception, manipulation, rejection, betrayal, abuse, torture, and violent death. No one truly understood him. He knows about loneliness. He is well acquainted with grief.

If he is God in human flesh, believing that he rose from the dead isn't a stretch for me. Rather, it seems plausible and natural. I believe he conquered death to offer me something better than the disappointment, pain, frustration, and loss of this world. I think he still conquers death, every day, in my life and in the lives of others.

Jesus knows. He knows grief, and he knows me. He shares my loneliness.

This companion has made all the difference for me. He shows up in interesting ways. He brings the right people at the right time, and loves me through them. His presence is constant. He reminds me this is not all there is. Death has been conquered.

I still have questions. I have doubts periodically, even about his goodness. I get mad at him occasionally. He accepts me where I am. He loves me. He gets it.

Again, this is my story. My prayer is that it brings some

comfort and hope to you in the midst of the current, inde-
scribable pain of losing a child. This is truly awful. There is
no other way to say it. Jesus knows. I believe he is in it with
you. He walks beside you in this valley of death.

I close with something Jesus himself said that has been
profoundly comforting to me. I hope you will find it so too.

---

*"Come to me, all you who are weary and burdened, and I will
give you rest. Take my yoke upon you and learn from me, for
I am gentle and humble of heart, and you will find rest for
your souls. For my yoke is easy and my burden is light."*

— *(Matthew 11:28-30)*

For more information about who Jesus is and what that
might mean for your life, grief process, and healing, please
visit www.garyroe.com/jesus-grief-and-healing

HELPFUL SCRIPTURES

HERE ARE SOME SCRIPTURES I have found comforting in times of grief, pain, and loss. Perhaps you will find them helpful and healing as well.

Be merciful to me, Lord, for I am in distress; my eyes grow weak with sorrow, my soul and body with grief.

— Psalm 31:9

Turn to me and be gracious to me, for I am lonely and afflicted.

— Psalm 25:16

But I trust in your unfailing love; my heart rejoices in your salvation.

— Psalm 13:5

The Lord is my shepherd, I lack nothing. He makes me lie down in green pastures, he leads me beside quiet waters, he refreshes my soul. He guides me along the right paths for his name's sake. Even though I walk through the darkest valley, I will fear no evil, for you are with me;

— Psalm 23:1-4

Surely your goodness and love will follow me all the days of my life, and I will dwell in the house of the Lord forever.

— Psalm 23:6

I remain confident of this: I will see the goodness of the Lord in the land of the living. Wait for the Lord; be strong and take heart and wait for the Lord.

— Psalm 27:13-14

I will be glad and rejoice in your love, for you saw my affliction and knew the anguish of my soul.

— Psalm 31:7

The Lord is close to the brokenhearted and saves those who are crushed in spirit.

— Psalm 34:18

As the deer pants for streams of water, so my soul pants for you, my God.

— Psalm 42:1

Why, my soul, are you downcast? Why so disturbed within me? Put your hope in God, for I will yet praise him, my Savior and my God.

— Psalm 42:11

God is our refuge and strength, an ever-present help in trouble. Therefore we will not fear, though the earth give way and the

mountains fall into the heart of the sea, though its waters
roar and foam and the mountains quake with their surging.

-Psalm 46:1-3

He says, "Be still, and know that I am God."

— Psalm 46:10

For great is your love, reaching to the heavens;
your faithfulness reaches to the skies.

— Psalm 57:10

You, God, are my God, earnestly I seek you; I
thirst for you, my whole being longs for you,
in a dry and parched land where there is no water.

— Psalm 63:1

My flesh and my heart may fail, but God is the
strength of my heart and my portion forever.

— Psalm 73:26

Unless the Lord had given me help, I would soon have dwelt
in the silence of death. When I said, "My foot is slipping,"
your unfailing love, Lord, supported me. When anxiety
was great within me, your consolation brought me joy.

— Psalm 94:17-19

He heals the brokenhearted and binds up their wounds.

— Psalm 147:3

So do not fear, for I am with you; do not be dismayed,
for I am your God. I will strengthen you and help you;
I will uphold you with my righteous right hand.

— Isaiah 41:10

He was despised and forsaken of men, a man of sorrows and
acquainted with grief; and like one from whom men hide
their face He was despised, and we did not esteem Him.

— Isaiah 53:3

You who are my Comforter in sorrow,
my heart is faint within me.

— Jer. 8:18

"For I know the plans I have for you," declares
the Lord, "plans to prosper you and not to harm
you, plans to give you hope and a future.

— Jer. 29:11

Because of the Lord's great love we are not consumed,
for his compassions never fail. They are new
every morning; great is your faithfulness.

— Lamentations 3:22-23

And we know that in all things God works for the good of those
who love him, who have been called according to his purpose.

— Romans 8:28

For I am convinced that neither death nor life, neither angels nor demons, neither the present nor the future, nor any powers, neither height nor depth, nor anything else in all creation, will be able to separate us from the love of God that is in Christ Jesus our Lord.

— Romans 8:38-39

Praise be to the God and Father of our Lord Jesus Christ, the Father of compassion and the God of all comfort, who comforts us in all our troubles, so that we can comfort those in any trouble with the comfort we ourselves receive from God.

— 2 Cor. 1:3-4

For just as we share abundantly in the sufferings of Christ, so also our comfort abounds through Christ.

— 2 Cor. 1:5

This is love: not that we loved God, but that he loved us and sent his Son as an atoning sacrifice for our sins.

— 1 John 4:10

And so we know and rely on the love God has for us. God is love.

— 1 John 4:16

'He will wipe every tear from their eyes. There will be no more death' or mourning or crying or pain, for the old order of things has passed away."

— Rev. 21:4

FROM THE WORDS OF JESUS:

"Blessed are the poor in spirit, for theirs is the kingdom of heaven. Blessed are those who mourn, for they will be comforted."

— Matt. 5:3-4

"See that you do not despise one of these little ones. For I tell you that their angels in heaven always see the face of my Father in heaven."

— Matthew 18:10

He said to them, "Let the little children come to me, and do not hinder them, for the kingdom of God belongs to such as these. Truly I tell you, anyone who will not receive the kingdom of God like a little child will never enter it."

— Mark 10:13-15

"For God so loved the world that he gave his one and only Son, that whoever believes in him shall not perish but have eternal life."

— John 3:16

"I am the good shepherd. The good shepherd lays down his life for the sheep."

— John 10:11

"Do not let your hearts be troubled. You believe in God; believe also in me."

— John 14:1

"I have told you these things, so that in me you may have peace. In this world you will have trouble. But take heart! I have overcome the world."

— John 16:33

HINTS FOR GROUP DISCUSSION

"CAN I USE THIS BOOK in a support group? If so, how?"

Great question. The answer is, "Yes!" Here are some guidelines.

GROUND RULES

First, make sure your group is clear on its purpose and rules of interaction. Here are my personal group ground rules that I read out loud at the beginning of each support group meeting.

GROUP GROUND RULES

We are hurting. We're here to support each other. Our losses are different, but we can walk together.

In order to grieve, share, and heal, we need to feel safe. As a result, here are our ground rules:

1. What is shared here is confidential. What is said in the group stays in the group.

2. We will not try to fix or help each other feel better. There is no fixing this.

3. We will not give advice unless someone specifically asks for input.

4. We will not compare our losses. There is no "easier," "harder," "better," or "worse," but only "different."

5. Each person is free to share. Each person is free not to share.

6. We will respect each other by being careful not to dominate, giving others a chance to share their story.

Having good, clear ground rules sets the tone for a good group.

TIME, PACING, AND DURATION

Second, if you're wanting to use *Shattered* in a support group, I would recommend having people read five chapters a week. Chapters 1-5 for the first week, chapters 6-10 for the second week, and so on. At that pace, it would take ten weeks to move through the book.

Also, I would personally recommend meeting weekly (continuity is important) for an hour and a half. This gives people a chance to settle, share, and support each other. Often the time after the group is equally valuable. Just being together can be profoundly helpful and healing.

SAMPLE QUESTIONS FOR GROUP MEETINGS

Third, here are sample questions (which I have tested) which tend to work well in most groups. You can even ask exactly the same questions each week. Some members like this because they know what's coming.

SAMPLE GENERALIZED QUESTIONS
FOR EACH WEEK

- Which of the five chapters from this week hit home the most with you? Why? Tell us about it.

- Was there an exercise from this week's chapters that was particularly helpful or difficult? Tell us about it.

- What do you sense was the most important thing you learned this week?

- Is there something you want to try this week to honor your child by grieving in a healthier way?

Remember that support groups are about people's hearts and lives, and not simply about getting through the material. Give the group direction. Be okay with silence, and yet keep them moving. Be intentional, and yet flexible. There is no "perfect" here. If you lead in a compassionate and loving way, you can bet that people will benefit.

Both leading and participating in support groups takes courage. You are braver than you know. Your child is worth it. You are worth it. Those around you are worth it.

A REQUEST FROM
THE AUTHOR

THANK YOU FOR TAKING YOUR heart seriously and reading *Shattered: Surviving the Loss of a Child.* I hope you found some comfort and healing in its pages.

I would love to hear what you thought of the book. Would you consider taking a moment and sending me a few sentences on how *Shattered* impacted you or helped in your grief process?

Send me your thoughts at contact@garyroe.com.

Your comments and feedback mean a lot to me, and will assist me in producing more quality resources for grieving hearts.

Thank you.

Warmly,
Gary

CARING FOR GRIEVING HEARTS

Visit Gary at www.garyroe.com and connect with him on Facebook, Twitter, LinkedIn, and Pinterest
Links:
Facebook: https://www.facebook.com/garyroeauthor
Twitter: https://twitter.com/GaryRoeAuthor
LinkedIn: https://www.linkedin.com/in/garyroeauthor
Pinterest: https://www.pinterest.com/garyroe79/

ADDITIONAL RESOURCES

BOOKS

Please Be Patient, I'm Grieving: How to Care For and Support the Grieving Heart

People often feel misunderstood, judged, and even rejected during a time of loss. This makes matters more difficult for an already broken heart. It doesn't have to be this way. It's time we took the grieving heart seriously. Gary wrote this book by request to help others better understand and support grieving hearts, and to help grieving hearts to understand themselves. A group discussion guide is included. *Please Be Patient, I'm Grieving* became a #1 Amazon Bestseller soon after its release and was honored as a 2016 Best Book Awards Finalist. It can be found in both paperback and electronic formats on Amazon and most other major online bookstores.

Surviving the Holidays Without You: Navigating Loss During Special Seasons

This warm and intensely practical volume has been dubbed a "Survival Kit for Holidays." It has helped many understand why holidays are especially hard while grieving and how to navigate them with greater confidence. Being proactive and having a plan can make all the difference. An Amazon holiday bestseller, *Surviving the Holidays*

Without You was a 2016 Book Excellence Award Finalist. Available in paperback and ebook formats on Amazon and most major online retailers.

Saying Goodbye: Facing the Loss of a Loved One

Full of stories, this warm, easy-to-read, and beautifully illustrated gift book has comforted thousands. It reads like a conversation with a close friend, giving wise counsel and hope to those facing a loss. Co-authored with *New York Times' Bestseller* Cecil Murphey, this attractive hardback edition is available at www.garyroe.com/saying-goodbye.

FREE ON GARY'S WEBSITE

The Good Grief Mini-Course

Full of personal stories, inspirational content, and practical assignments, this 8-session mini-course is designed to help readers understand grief and deal with its roller-coaster emotions. Several thousand have been through this course, which is now being used in support groups as well. Available at www.garyroe.com/good-grief

The Hole in My Heart: Tackling Grief's Tough Questions

This new, powerful e-book tackles some of grief's big questions: "How did this happen?" "Why?" "Am I crazy?" "Am I normal?" "Will this get any easier?" plus others. Written in the first person, it engages and comforts the heart. Available at www.garyroe.com/theholeinmyheart

I Miss You: A Holiday Survival Kit

Thousands have downloaded this brief, easy-to-read, and very personal e-book. *I Miss You* provides some basic, simple tools on how to use holidays and special times to grieve well and love those around you. Available at www. garyroe.com/imissyou

ABOUT THE AUTHOR

GARY'S STORY BEGAN WITH A childhood of mixed messages and sexual abuse. This was followed by other losses and numerous grief experiences.

Ultimately, a painful past led Gary into a life of helping wounded people heal and grow. A former college minister, missionary in Japan, entrepreneur in Hawaii, and pastor in Texas and Washington, he now serves as a writer, speaker, chaplain, and grief specialist with Hospice Brazos Valley in central Texas.

In addition to *Shattered: Surviving the Loss of a Child*, Gary is the author of five books, including the award-winning Amazon Bestsellers *Please Be Patient, I'm Grieving*, *Heartbroken: Healing from the Loss of a Spouse* and *Surviving the Holidays Without You*. He is also the co-author (with *New York Times* Bestseller Cecil Murphey) of *Not Quite Healed* and *Saying Goodbye*. Gary has been featured on Focus on the Family and CBN, and has more than 400 grief-related articles in print. He is a popular speaker at a wide variety of venues.

Gary loves being a husband and father. He has seven adopted children, including three Colombian daughters. He enjoys swimming, hockey, corny jokes, and cool Hawaiian shirts. Gary and his wife Jen and family live in Texas. Visit him at www.garyroe.com and follow him on Facebook, Twitter, LinkedIn, and Pinterest.

Links:
Facebook: https://www.facebook.com/garyroeauthor
Twitter: https://twitter.com/GaryRoeAuthor
LinkedIn: https://www.linkedin.com/in/garyroeauthor
Pinterest: https://www.pinterest.com/garyroe79/

Made in the USA
Lexington, KY
16 October 2018